UNCERTAIN GROUND

ALSO BY PHIL KLAY

Redeployment
Missionaries

UNCERTAIN GROUND

CITIZENSHIP IN AN AGE OF ENDLESS, INVISIBLE WAR

PHIL KLAY

Penguin Press ‖ *New York*
2022

PENGUIN PRESS
An imprint of Penguin Random House LLC
penguinrandomhouse.com

The essays in this book were originally published 2010–2021.

"The Good War" was previously published in *The Daily Beast*.

"The Lesson of Eric Greitens, and the Navy SEALs Who Tried to Warn Us," "American Purpose After the Fall of Kabul," and "A History of Violence" were previously published in *The New Yorker*.

"Fact and Fiction" was written for the International Literary Festival Erich Fried Days, Vienna; published in *Kolik* No. 67, 2015.

"Citizen-Soldier" was previously published in the Brookings Institution's Brookings Essay Series.

"Death and Memory," "What We're Fighting For," "The Warrior at the Mall," "The Soldiers We Leave Behind," "After War, a Failure of the Imagination," and "Can the Trauma of War Lead to Growth, Despite the Scars?" were previously published in *The New York Times*.

"Fear and Loathing in Mosul" was previously published in *American Affairs*.

"Left Behind" was previously published in *The Atlantic*.

"Man of War" was previously published in *America* magazine.

"Duty and Pity" was previously published in *The Wall Street Journal*.

"We Have No Idea What We're Doing in Iraq. We Didn't Before We Killed Suleimani" was previously published in *The Washington Post*.

"Public Rage Won't Solve Any of Our Problems" was previously published in *Time* magazine.

"Tales of War and Redemption" was previously published in *The American Scholar*.

"How We Mourned, Why We Fought" and "War, Loss, and Unthinkable Youth" were previously published in the *New York Daily News*.

"Visions of War and Peace: Literature and Authority in World War I" was previously published by *The World War One Centennial Commission Write Blog*.

LIBRARY OF CONGRESS CATALOGING-IN-PUBLICATION DATA
Names: Klay, Phil, author.
Title: Uncertain ground : citizenship in an age of endless, invisible war / Phil Klay.
Description: New York : Penguin Press, 2022. | Includes index.
Identifiers: LCCN 2021027476 (print) | LCCN 2021027477 (ebook) |
ISBN 9780593299241 (hardcover) | ISBN 9780593299258 (ebook)
Subjects: LCSH: Klay, Phil. | United States. Marine Corps—Biography. |
Civil-military relations—United States. | War and society—United States. |
United States—Armed Forces—Public opinion. | United States—Military policy—Public opinion. | United States--Social conditions—21st century. | United States—Politics and government—2009-2017. | United States—Politics and government—2017-2021.
Classification: LCC JK330 .K53 2022 (print) | LCC JK330 (ebook) |
DDC 359.9/60973—dc23/eng/20211130
LC record available at https://lccn.loc.gov/2021027476
LC ebook record available at https://lccn.loc.gov/2021027477

Printed in the United States of America
10 9 8 7 6 5 4 3 2 1

BOOK DESIGN BY LUCIA BERNARD

For Adrian, Marcos, and Lucas

CONTENTS

INTRODUCTION

I n 2009, when the Global War on Terror was in its eighth year, twice
as long as America spent fighting World War II, a high school student named Javier J. Gutierrez headed off to the army. Like I had
been, he was young and idealistic and full of faith, in America and in
God. "It was his sense of calling from his Heavenly Father that he
pursued the military life," his obituary would one day read. And upon
graduating from basic training, the newly minted eighteen-year-old
private had put on his uniform and gone to the hospital to visit his
great-grandfather, a bombardier in the Army Air Forces who'd been
shot down and taken prisoner by the Nazis. The old man, a veteran of
our most celebrated military triumph, could no longer talk. Still, he
had wept at the sight.

I was leaving the Marine Corps then, and though I was only
twenty-five, the youth of new Marines and soldiers started getting to

me. Baby-faced children heading out on deployments, coming back a little harder, leaner, but kids nonetheless. The protective eyewear they'd used on deployment would create ridiculous tan lines around their eyes, leaving them looking like a pack of scruffy, underfed racoons. Back in 2009, I was still hopeful about the missions we were sending those kids out on. The surge of troops to Iraq that I'd been a part of had succeeded in lowering the level of violence there, and President Barack Obama was pushing for a similar strategy in Afghanistan. Maybe things really would wind down soon.

And so, as I started writing about the war and the people who fight it, I envisioned my task primarily as making sense of the past. But the Global War on Terror, begun in Afghanistan and Iraq but soon expanding to Syria and Somalia and Pakistan and the Philippines, wouldn't stay behind me. Unlike Gutierrez's father's war, which ended with the declaration of a cease-fire and the liberation of Kuwait on February 28, 1991, and his great-grandfather's war, which ended on September 2, 1945, my war just kept going.

Gutierrez would serve in Iraq, get married, and have four kids in between deployments and training exercises. He'd join the 7th Special Forces Group, an elite unit intended to focus on Latin America, but which has sent Green Beret teams on an endless series of deployments to Afghanistan. There he'd meet Antonio Rodriguez, who had also joined the military out of high school in 2009, and who was heading out on his tenth deployment to Afghanistan in as many years.

During the two men's decade in service, the wars would warp and change. Instead of large numbers of troops, we shifted to smaller deployments of highly specialized forces, buttressed by the support of mercenaries and military contractors who in some places outnumbered active-duty troops three to one. This kept casualties low. So on February 8, 2020,

Gutierrez and Rodriguez would become the last American soldiers to fall in combat prior to the final, tragic evacuation.

The men received heroes' burials back in their hometowns. Schoolchildren in Las Cruces, New Mexico, lined the street and waved flags across from the church holding Rodriguez's funeral Mass. Police and firefighters stood at attention as the casket passed, hundreds of community members joining in the mourning. You can watch videos online of the broad turnout at Gutierrez's funeral, including, if you can stand the sadness of it, footage of his wife and four small children receiving the flag from his casket. His obituary notes that he "lived sacrificially for his family."

Outside of their hometowns, though, the deaths received hardly any notice from a public whose interest in the Global War on Terror had vanished years before. That indifference had become emblematic of the wars the two men fought in, as was the nature of their deaths, which didn't come while raiding a compound, or hitting an improvised explosive device, but when an American-trained Afghan soldier turned his American-supplied machine gun on American backs. A final irony was their mission at the time: a "key-leader engagement" in Nangarhar Province. Yet another attempt, twenty years into the war, to win allies among the locals.

How to speak meaningfully of a conflict that has lasted so long, and at such a low ebb that most Americans can pretend it isn't happening? "No one cares if Americans aren't being killed," the journalist Jonah Goldberg recently argued, "nor should they care if Americans aren't being killed." As far as public opinion goes, he's largely right.

And yet, whether or not war still captures the attention of the public, it still captures the attention of the Defense Department, which continues long-running and extremely lethal campaigns in various theaters of conflict. We may not be *losing* as many soldiers as we used to, since our role in wars has shifted to one of training, support, and the provision of airpower and high-tech know-how, but we're certainly killing plenty of people.

Nor are the dead and injured just members of terrorist groups. In 2020, so blissfully low in U.S. casualties in Afghanistan, the UN has tracked 120 civilian casualties that can be directly tied to international security forces. This somewhat understates our lethal presence in the region. The U.S.-trained and -supplied Afghan Air Force caused a further 693 civilian casualties, while the Afghan security forces as a whole caused 1,906. When they died, Afghanistan was a deadlier place for civilians than when Gutierrez and Rodriguez were graduating high school.

And though we have removed our ground troops, our lethal presence remains in the skies above. In the same speech where President Biden claimed to have ended twenty years of war, he announced "we will maintain the fight against terrorism in Afghanistan and other countries," by relying on over-the-horizon capabilities instead of ground troops. The war was over, supposedly, but not the killing.

What this means in practice is not simply children losing parents who lived sacrificially for their families, but also, since Afghanistan is one of the deadliest places in the world to be a child, parents losing children. The most recent UN report on civilian casualties in Afghanistan quotes the father of a boy killed in September 2020 by an "explosive remnant of war," a bomb fragment left behind by one side or the other. He remembers hearing children screaming, "Please help us," then seeing his son and four others, all grievously wounded. "I took my son," he said. "There was blood all over his body." Stomach, heart, and lungs had all been pierced, wounds that meant death within minutes. The father took water and tried to clean the injuries. "When he died," the man said, "he was looking toward me, straight into my eyes, but unable to speak."

So yes, even though in America we're swaddled from the consequences, we're still at war. Wherever we're regularly killing, we're at war. Which leads to the increasingly complex question of *where* we're killing people. Iraq, Syria, Yemen, Somalia, Pakistan, and Libya—for those places the answer is certainly "yes." Brian Castner, a former Explosive Ordnance Disposal tech now at Amnesty International, tells me, "I can give you strike by strike in Somalia, because the military at least acknowledges those strikes." But then there are other countries he describes as a "true black box," like Niger, Mali, and Nigeria. "We know when U.S. soldiers die in Niger," he says. "We don't know when the U.S. kills people in Niger."

Talking about American wars, then, increasingly becomes like talking about Schrödinger's cat. Outside the closed black boxes of our military involvement overseas, the American public remains blissfully at peace until an American dies, and it turns out we were at war all along.

No wonder we've turned inward, especially when images of conflict can strike much closer to home. Like the death of another veteran, Ashli Babbitt, one that happened in far less honorable, and even more darkly tragic circumstances. Babbitt, who served two tours of duty in Afghanistan, was one of a disturbingly large number of veterans present at the storming of the U.S. Capitol Building on January 6, 2021. After having previously voted for Barack Obama, she became a Trump supporter and follower of the QAnon conspiracy theory, ultimately joining the crowd that broke into the Capitol, beating and

injuring police officers and storming the halls of Congress only moments after the chambers had been evacuated. "Nothing will stop us,"
she had written in a social media post the day before. "They can try
and try and try but the storm is here and it is descending upon DC."
She was shot while climbing onto a ledge near a locked door the insurrectionists were trying to get through. This video can also be found
online.

What a thrill it must have been for Babbitt in the moments before
she died. How much more meaningful than the frustrating, indeter-
minate war she fought in it must have been to have a simple, clear
enemy, and a simple, clear mission—to take Congress and make them
reinstate President Trump by force.

It's easy to dismiss Babbitt as a loon, but her beliefs were a distilled,
paranoid version of a not-so-unreasonable distrust of American elites.
The past decades of war have shown mismanagement, incompetence,
bald-faced lies, as well as forms of cruelty only a bit less bizarre than
QAnon, such as the CIA's use of hummus enemas as a form of torture.
The sense that our leadership class can be corrupt, or ineffectual, or
malevolent, or callous, or blindly self-interested, is well founded.

The power of that distrust was driven home for me a few weeks
before the 2016 election. I was driving through rural Cambria County,
Pennsylvania, on the way to the wedding of a friend from the Corps.
The coal-country landscape was breathtakingly beautiful and dotted
with "Trump Digs Coal" signs. My Colombian American wife, half
jokingly, half nervously, asked if she would be the only Hispanic in
attendance. "No, it's a military guy's wedding, it'll be super diverse," I
told her, a prediction that turned out to be correct. And the day of the
wedding, as I was helping the groom prepare, I sent my wife a text
message that read: "You're actually not the only Hispanic at the wedding. You're not even the only Colombian." And then I followed it up

with this: "The other groomsman is half Cuban, half Colombian, and he voted early for Trump."

His rationale was straightforward. "We're both Marines," he told me. "We both know guys who have been killed, or horribly injured, overseas. And for what?" Iraq was in chaos. Afghanistan was continuing its slow deterioration. Our military adventurism had been a human catastrophe for the countries we'd invaded.

"And Hillary is a hawk," he said. Which is true. She has a long track record of supporting military interventions or expanding them. She'd pushed for more troops for Obama's surge in Afghanistan than the secretary of defense had, promoted regime change in Libya, and argued for increased military aid to Syrian rebels. "Does Donald Trump have a good understanding of the military? Probably not," he admitted. But Trump had been far more resistant to expanding America's military footprint than Hillary. The groomsman preferred even an incompetent and inconstant resistance to our wars over the competent expansion of them, since the downside of the latter could be measured in tens of thousands if not hundreds of thousands of lives.

It wasn't the last time I'd hear similar sentiments. "If Trump gets us out of the Middle East, I might vote for him," one usually left-leaning veteran told me toward the end of 2019.

The most passionate argument I heard for continued U.S. presence overseas that year came not from an American, but from a Syrian refugee living in a camp with his pregnant wife and two small children. Trump's partial pullout of U.S. troops from the region had opened the space for Turkish-backed militias, which had brutalized the local population. When I asked how his children were handling life in the camp, his wife started crying. "They cry all the time, asking to go home. It wasn't even good back home. Now he's wounded, I'm pregnant, and it is too much to take care of everyone." The man left little doubt as to who he felt was responsible. "The U.S. left for its own good. Kurds held hands with the U.S. to fight ISIS," he said. "The Turkish militia is way worse than ISIS. They kill, steal, and destroy homes. The U.S. should go back to Syria and stop Erdogan from killing the elderly, from killing children."

But such appeals for and against war are only of existential importance to combatants and to civilian victims. Until Afghanistan's final, dramatic collapse, news of the Taliban encircling key cities in Afghanistan barely elicited a shrug from the collective body politic. And now, looking at the images of the violence wrought on January 6 by Ashli Babbitt and her fellow insurrectionists, the cops screaming in pain, the insurrectionists beating police officers with American and Trump flags, the realization strikes me that the most prominent images of anything resembling war in years were images of Americans killing each other.

Tragically and farcically, the wars have come home. Unable to find an overseas enemy who'll allow us to definitively vanquish him, our greatest fears have become each other.

THIS CREATES a bizarre circumstance for Americans trying to understand their citizenship, and their humanity, in relation to the killing done in our name. War remains a large part of who we are as Americans, with almost a sixth of our federal budget going to defense, keeping troops deployed in eight hundred military bases around the world and engaging in counterterror missions in eighty-five countries. And yet, thanks to a series of political and strategic choices, to the average American that's mostly invisible.

During my past decade of writing about war, I've often been unsure of whether I'm fulfilling a civic obligation, exploring a personal obsession, accepting a religious duty, or simply screaming into the void. While a decade ago Obama's opposition to the Iraq War had been a major factor in his beating Hillary Clinton to the presidency, in the last presidential cycle, our long-running wars got barely a mention in the presidential debates between Joe Biden and Donald Trump. The candidates, along with most of our major thinkers and writers, remained focused inward, not outward. Donald Trump may no longer be president, but when it comes to Americans thinking through their place in the world, it's his slogan that has triumphed: America First.

The essays in this book represent my attempts, over the course of the Obama and Trump administrations, to grapple with how we got here. Questions about what my experience of war meant for me personally, and what can be genuinely communicated about war across differences, steadily shifted into questions of what our wars say about us as Americans, how they have distorted our politics and culture, and how our politics have shifted to shield our wars from our view. And then there are deeper concerns about how the experience of war relates to questions of faith, how we respond to collective and individual trauma, and how to reckon with guilt and atonement.

It has been an often frustrating, though not entirely dispiriting, enterprise. I still have faith in the American promise, and hope for the next generation of warfighters, who even now are getting ready to graduate high school or college and offer their bodies to the United States of America. Though the past two decades of American wars have destroyed the innocent idealism that initially inspired me to join the military, I'd like to think a different, tougher form of idealism remains. "Break a vase," the poet Derek Walcott proclaimed, "and the love that reassembles the fragments is stronger than that love which took its symmetry for granted when it was whole." These essays consist of so many broken fragments of my faith in, and love of, America.

I | SOLDIERS

DEATH AND MEMORY

OCTOBER 28, 2010

When I tell stories about Iraq, the ones people react to are always the stories of violence. This is strange for me. As a public affairs officer in 2007 and 2008, I never saw combat, only its aftermath. I saw women and children wounded or dying in trauma centers. Ruins left by explosives in towns and cities across Anbar Province. I saw surgeons who could do no more because the body they were trying to repair was too badly destroyed. I stood in formations as the bodies were taken away.

And when I try to describe that death, the telling tends to decay into a kind of pornographic, voyeuristic experience. I feel I do disservice to the enormity of my subject by making it a subject of conversation. And yet I know that keeping a hushed silence is a failure, too, because by not telling these stories we fail to process them.

Most of the suffering I have seen has not affected me as it should have. While I was in Iraq, I never cried over the bloody children I helped carry to the navy doctors, or the two men who'd been tortured with drills through their ankles. Only one death out of the many gave me pause. It was of a Marine who died, not in front of me, but near me. Near enough for me to see it happen, had I been paying attention.

Midway through the summer of 2007, we had two Marines come in a CASEVAC from somewhere in Anbar. They'd been hit by an IED. I had one of my Marines, Corporal Thomas J. Griffith, who took photographs and wrote stories for the Marine Corps, at the desert trauma center documenting our medical personnel at work, so he was there with his camera. I was there, too, talking with the medical staff and checking in on a journalist we had embedded with us.

As the injured Marines were brought in, one of them managed to put his fingers up in a victory sign. Grif snapped a shot. Both were hustled to the trauma tables and surrounded by a sea of surgeons and navy corpsmen. They'd have to amputate one leg—the leg of the Marine who didn't mug for the camera. While they were working, they got word that another one was coming in, and that CPR had already started on the bird. That was a bad sign. They say if you make it to a trauma table with a pulse, you'll probably pull through. So the docs were hoping his heart would get there still beating.

They brought him in and cracked him open, trying to restart his heart. A crowd of people were working on him, but Grif managed clean shots of the docs, the chaplain, and others. He left the dying Marine alone.

While this was going on, I know I was around somewhere, but I can't remember where exactly. I know I wasn't involved in any kind of deep feeling about it. I was busy. There's a lot to focus on in a trauma ward, and death happens with a certain degree of regularity, though it had been declining in recent months and would soon drop precipitously. And of course, it's difficult to relate to the inner contents of another person's chest. I've had cuts, abrasions, and lacerations. I saw a child's face riddled with shrapnel once, and I could relate to that damage. I could take the sight before me and turn it into an idea of how badly traumatized the human body that I was observing must have been. And then I could feel horror. But an open chest, the skin stretched unnaturally to enable access, instruments poking among the organs, that's like nothing in my experience. If you knew that Marine, I suppose the sight would be terrible, seeing your buddy, your squad member, looking like this. Hardly like a person. If you didn't know the Marine, nothing.

So I was in and out. But for the docs, this was a person. They know what that trauma means to a human body. And they worked until the head surgeon, who had his hands deep in the Marine's chest, stopped. He raised a hand, bladed, signaling that there was no more to be done. Grif snapped the shot.

I would never have thought about that Marine again, except for Grif's photos. Grif assembled them and turned them into an audio slideshow, and when I had a spare minute I sat down at my desk in Al Taqaddum and really looked at them. I saw the images and heard Grif's recorded voice over them. When he announced the death of the unnamed Marine, I found myself looking at a photo of the surgeon, his hand falling away from his neck but his eyes fixed in front of him, out at his fellow sailors.

It was at this moment, in the quiet time I had created for myself to review my Marines' work, that a surge of emotion swept over me, something I couldn't shake, and still can't. I recall the details of the day, half noticed at the time. Like the corpsman wiping up blood on the floor, and there is too much and now there are just red streaks in an arc like a monochromatic rainbow. And spattered blood drops.

And dust. The one Marine so surrounded and obscured by medical equipment I couldn't see his face, only a tattoo of a cross on his right shoulder, and an eagle, globe, and anchor beneath a four-leaf clover on his breast.

The only time I had anything even remotely resembling a flashback had to do with that Marine. I was given two weeks' leave midway through my deployment, and I went home to New York. At one point I walked down Madison Avenue, near where it intersects with Broadway. It was a beautiful day. The sun was shining off the Flatiron Building, men and women were passing by in summer clothes, and I was seized without warning by the urge to weep. The images came back not as photographs, but as living memories. And for that moment Madison Avenue seemed just a fiction, one that was lovely but spun so thin I could see through it, to the desert where that Marine fought and died.

THE FIERCENESS OF my recollection and the emotions that come with it have everything to do with seeing those photos and hearing Grif's voice tell the story. It is not because I was there. When a suicide bomber killed over thirty people outside our gate and we brought the wounded into surgical, I helped carry an injured child and thought, "I will never forget this kid's face." It was the first brutally injured child I had ever seen in my life. By the end of the night, I couldn't have picked him out of a lineup. By that time I had seen too many injured children, been too busy for emotional indulgences. And no one told me that child's story later, in a time of quiet.

We're told that when we remember, the same parts of our brain light up as when we experienced the event we're remembering. Your brain lives through it again. But here, watching Grif's piece, I experienced it for the first time.

I'm not sure what the unnamed Marine would say if he knew the emotions his death sparked in me, if he would mock me for their artificiality, reject any sympathy from someone who could not hope to understand what he experienced. Though I continue to tell stories about Iraq, I sometimes fear this makes me a fraud. I feel guilty about the sorrow I feel because I know it is manufactured, and I feel guilty about the sorrow I do not feel because it is owed, it is the barest beginning of what is owed to the fallen.

HOW WE MOURNED, WHY
WE FOUGHT

SEPTEMBER 11, 2011

The day Osama bin Laden died, I learned one of my former Marines was permanently blind. He was recovering from an IED strike and I'd called to check in. Months back they'd said his vision loss was temporary. As it turned out, he'd regained peripheral vision, but no more. The Corps had trained him as a journalist. Now he couldn't read.

Three hours later I learned bin Laden was dead: news that should have felt like closure, but didn't. One of my Marines was blind, and though I wanted to tie in Osama's death and 9/11 to make sense of it, I couldn't.

When my Marine was hit, he was in Afghanistan as part of President Obama's surge. That strategy was predicated on the success of the Iraq surge, itself an outgrowth of previous Iraq policy. Further muddling things, the Iraq War necessitated the drawdown in

Afghanistan in 2003, which shaped the environment where my Marine was injured.

These policies didn't derive solely from 9/11. They derived from presidential leadership, and the will of the American people. And though the specter of 9/11 might have been used to justify those policies, we shouldn't confuse the complex legacy of 9/11 with 9/11 itself.

That day three thousand people died, a number that for many Americans is as abstract as our thirty-seven thousand yearly traffic fatalities, but for New Yorkers it is not abstract at all. We knew the dead. We know the still-suffering living. For one friend, 9/11 is the day his mother came home covered in ash and wouldn't talk about it for months. For another, it's what turned her first-responder father into a different, sadder man.

September 11 was the Hasidic men and children handing out bottles of water to people fleeing Manhattan over the Williamsburg Bridge. It was the man who bought coffee for a young, exhausted cop, only to see the cop break down crying. It was the days after—all those 9/12s. The pictures in the subway: "Have you seen my brother?" "Have you seen my daughter?" For New Yorkers, it's personal.

The specter of 9/11, though, is as impersonal as an airport body scan. It's not an individual story, but a vague sense of approaching doom. It's a somber ghost hanging over our national discourse, unassailable, draped in a tattered U.S. flag, and repetitively moaning about America under attack.

I'm a New Yorker. My parents took me to the top of the Twin Towers when I was a child. After 9/11, I walked to Ground Zero at night and saw twisted metal and fog, but no clear way to help. Within three years I'd joined the Marine Corps. Within six, I was in Iraq. There I saw Marines work tirelessly to heal the damage done by sectarian divisions, but I came home to a nation where the specter of 9/11 has taken us in the other direction. We're so frightened we make American Muslims endure months of spurious legal challenges before they can build a mosque, and more than a dozen states are considering legislation opposing sharia law.

When my Marine told me he was blind, I focused on his loss. He looked to the future. This year, he might make staff sergeant. And for next year, he's challenged me to a grappling match. The other day he told me he's been working out. Apparently, I'm in trouble. None of this means he's forgotten the day of his injuries, or the sacrifices of his fellow Marines, but his life doesn't revolve around them any more than ours should revolve around 9/11.

If you go to downtown Manhattan, you'll see Ground Zero. But you'll also see a vibrant neighborhood coalescing around the scars. This is as it should be. New York has recovered, though the specter of 9/11 continues to haunt the nation at large. Perhaps with the tenth anniversary of 9/11, we'll be able to exorcise it for good.

LEFT BEHIND

South of Fallujah's Route Fran were hundreds of insurgents who'd spent months digging trench lines, emplacing roadside bombs, barricading streets, training with their weapons, reading the Koran, and watching videos of suicide bombers to inspire them for the fight to come. North of Route Fran were the roughly one thousand men of 1st Battalion, 8th Marine Regiment, preparing themselves for the assault. Route Fran itself was a wide, four-lane highway. On November 9, 2004, the highway was wet—it'd rained the previous day—and the sky was gray and foreboding.

"You just know that this whole company crossing this road," Marine Justin Best later told a reporter, "someone's gonna get hit."

When crossing an open space like Fran, it's important to have units in overwatch, shooting at locations from which the enemy might fire at you and your buddies. Most of the bullets expended in war aren't intended to kill the enemy so much as to keep his head down while you maneuver your way to a place where you *can* kill him. It doesn't always work. There were enough large buildings on either side of Fran that the Marines could never hope to cover every window.

The Marines started to cross—one platoon running at full speed, the others firing away, filling the sky above with bullets. Insurgents on the other side opened up as well, one of them hitting Sergeant Lonny Wells, a twenty-nine-year-old father of four children. The round tore through his leg and he pitched forward, falling to the ground. Wells, his mother later recalled, had wanted to join the military since he was young. She'd tell him, "Why don't you try to be a model? You've got the looks." And he'd reply, "Oh, Mom, I'm gonna be a Marine." Now he was facedown in the middle of an open highway in Fallujah, blood pooling around his body.

Gunnery Sergeant Ryan Shane, whose platoon had been providing covering fire, put down his rifle. As a senior leader, he wasn't expected to be the one to recover Wells. Nevertheless, he ran out to the fallen Marine, grabbed him by the drag strap on his body armor, and along with one other Marine, began tugging him to safety. After Shane took a few steps, a bullet slammed into his lower back, and he fell to the ground. Now there were two injured men facedown in the middle of the open highway, bleeding onto the wet pavement.

Everyone in overwatch had seen Wells fall, and they'd seen what had happened to Shane when he'd tried to help. They all must have known that the two injured men were now bait, that insurgents were waiting to fire on anyone else foolish enough to try to save their brothers. Naturally, Marines being Marines, two more of them ran out. Thanks to them, Shane would live, but they were too late for Wells. He bled to death.

This is a common sort of war story. Every war provides them— young men and women risking and sometimes losing their lives in ways that provoke a kind of entranced awe. How, and why, do they do it? In America, we have a very particular set of answers. Driving through the South, outside of churches you'll occasionally see a Fallen Soldier Battle Cross next to a sign bearing an image of Christ and a message: THEY BOTH DIED FOR YOUR FREEDOM. Ronald Reagan once posed the author James Michener's question about the heroes of the Korean War—"Where do we find such men?"—only to answer it with, "Well, we find them where we've always found them. They are the product of the freest society man has ever known."

In this view, ours is a democratic courage, the purest reflection of the nature and quality of our society. Those men who rushed out under fire were formed by our civic body. Raised in our American democracy, with its love of liberty, strong civic institutions, and glorious past, those men would fight courageously as, in George Washington's words, "Freemen" and not as "base hirelings and mercenaries."

In turn, we, as members of that body from which they came, are to take heart from their example and commit ourselves with equal vigor to sustaining an American civil society that will continue to inspire such courage. When Abraham Lincoln stood at Gettysburg, he channeled what he claimed were the democratic impulses of the Union dead, urging the nation to rededicate itself with "increased devotion to that cause for which they gave the last full measure of devotion." When Woodrow Wilson stood at the American Cemetery in Suresnes, France, he channeled the same impulses in articulating what he called the "unspoken mandates of our dead."

The fraternal bonds of combat have always been invoked to political ends. But as we stand on the edge of seventeen years of war, these ends have become smaller, indeed almost pathetic. When Donald Trump addressed the widow of a fallen Navy SEAL in the middle of a speech to Congress in February 2017, he didn't articulate a vision of American ideals, or outline our broader moral purpose in the world, but merely defended his claim that the raid in which the SEAL was killed had been a success, generating intelligence that would lead to more targets in the never-ending War on Terror. The president and the widow received rapturous applause. "He became president of the United States in that moment," one political commentator on CNN said, arguing that the president's deployment of the grieving widow was "unifying." If it was, the blood of the fallen SEAL proved a weak glue, lasting little longer than the bipartisan applause that briefly filled the Capitol Building.

"War will purify the political atmosphere," one magazine argued on the eve of the War of 1812, America's first great military disappointment. "All the public virtues will be refined and hallowed; and we shall again behold at the head of affairs citizens who may rival the immortal men of 1776." In our era of constant war, something like the opposite is happening. Though the military currently enjoys stratospheric approval ratings—72 percent of Americans express a "great deal" or "quite a lot" of confidence in it—almost every other major institution of American life is in the red: 12 percent approval for Congress, 27 percent for newspapers, 40 percent for the Supreme Court, and 41 percent for organized religion. Meanwhile, 27 percent of Democrats and 36 percent of Republicans see the opposing party as a threat to the nation.

If the courage of young men and women in battle truly does depend on the nature and quality of our civic society, we should be very worried. We should expect to see a sickness spreading from our public life and into the hearts of the men and women who continue to risk their lives on behalf of a distracted nation. And when we look closely, that is exactly what we see: a sickness that all the ritualistic displays of support for our troops at sporting events and Veterans Day celebrations, and in the halls of Congress, can't cure. Such tributes don't begin to get at what "the last full measure of devotion" actually means on the ground, or what might be required to sustain it. The bonds of men in combat are far stranger, and perhaps more fragile, than our lofty rhetoric would suggest.

IN 1999, Maurice Emerson Decaul was preparing to deploy overseas with a member of the Ku Klux Klan. Decaul, who is black, was a lance corporal in a Marine artillery battery. Because your average military unit is a cross section of American society, he might well have expected to work alongside a broad range of Americans—white kids from the northern Virginia suburbs, Hispanic kids from small towns in New Mexico, children of Vietnamese refugees from rural Indiana. More surprising, though, was the West Virginia kid from a family so deep in the Klan that he showed up to the battery's barracks with a hooded white robe packed in among his Marine Corps uniforms. I'll call him "J."

If Decaul had wanted to—if anybody in the unit had wanted to—he could have gotten J. booted out of the Corps. The Marines don't tolerate hate groups, and the service regularly runs classes on how to spot gang and hate-group tattoos to help officers identify and remove their members. When General Robert B. Neller, the commandant of the Marine Corps, tweeted out a condemnation of racial hatred and extremism in the wake of last year's neo-Nazi rally in Charlottesville, Virginia, he was giving voice to a policy that dated back to the 1980s. That policy was kicked into even higher gear after Timothy McVeigh, a Gulf War veteran, bombed the Alfred P. Murrah Federal Building in Oklahoma City. As far as the military was concerned, men like J.

didn't just undermine unit cohesion and the moral character of the force, they were also a domestic terror threat. If somebody had notified the chain of command, or even left an anonymous note at the office of the unit lawyer, the unit would have investigated, and that would have been that. Such things, a military lawyer told me, are a pretty straightforward affair. But this is not what happened.

Instead, J.'s fellow Marines observed him in training as they geared up for deployment. Even though it was pre-9/11, combat was a possibility. The previous unit to go on their planned deployment had ended up taking a detour to the Balkans. The leadership had impressed upon Decaul's unit that they might be relying on their fellow Marines for their lives. Which meant that Decaul and the rest of the black and Hispanic and Asian and Jewish kids might be relying on a Klansman, and not simply in a day-to-day "Can I trust this guy at the office?" kind of way. The question before a deploying Marine as he looks at his brothers and sisters is quite simple: *If I am, like Sergeant Wells and Gunny Shane, facedown and bleeding to death in the middle of an open highway as small-arms fire rages around me, will you run out to save my life?*

This might seem like a lot to expect of J., but Decaul didn't have any serious concerns. "I never felt like I couldn't trust J. in combat," Decaul told me, seeming a bit amazed by the words coming out of his mouth. "I never felt like J. didn't know his job. In training, you see who you can trust. You see the guys who shy away. And, well, he wasn't one of those guys."

J. wasn't the only racist Marine that Decaul dealt with while in the Corps. Once, during mountain training—a famously austere experience that Decaul told me was worse than his time in Iraq—he'd had to care for a lance corporal on his fire team who had developed altitude sickness. Because Decaul was this guy's noncommissioned officer, he helped the Marine make his slow and painful way down the mountain. Midway through, they stopped to rest, and the young Marine, perhaps out of an awkward sense of the gratitude his leader was owed, began telling Decaul about his family, and the racism he had been raised to believe in. It wasn't an apology. It was something short of that—an openness, a moment of honesty without the kind of moral epiphany such moments are supposed to bring about. He didn't attempt a racial reconcilement, he didn't beg forgiveness for a past that included his family's denial of Decaul's basic equality. Decaul listened to the lance corporal, who was his Marine and his responsibility, and then they continued down the mountain.

As a black man in America, Decaul could expect that being part of a national organization, be it the Marine Corps or any other, meant putting his shoulder to the wheel alongside the sort of people who in generations past had lynched and tortured men like himself. Nothing about this is just, but with a pragmatism that is common to members of the military, he accepted it and did his job. And he considered his unit's relationship to J. in the context of that job.

Just before the battery deployed, its members threw a big, blowout barracks party. For those who have never gone to a barracks party, or been the officer on duty responsible for dealing with the chaos that follows one, imagine a frat party but with almost no women and even less common sense. "We were nineteen; there was this feeling that maybe we could die," Decaul told me. "So fuck it, have fun, get that shit out of your system."

One sergeant started proclaiming that he was Batman. When fellow Marines called bullshit, the sergeant decided to prove the haters wrong by jumping off the third deck of the barracks. He broke both his legs. Apparently, he was not Batman. Another Marine, a lance corporal, led a high-speed, lights-off drunk drive to raid another barracks. But what Decaul remembers most vividly from that night is seeing J. appear on the barracks' catwalk in his Ku Klux Klan gear, hood and all.

Another black Marine made a beeline over to the West Virginian Klansman. He got right in J.'s face while everybody else watched, wondering what was about to happen in this confrontation between a black Marine and the embodiment of American white supremacy. "Hey," he said, staring into J.'s eyes, "let me wear your Klan suit." J. stripped off his robe and hood and handed them to the black Marine, who put them on and began walking around the party in the Klan uniform, giving people high fives and cracking jokes.

Decaul now has a playwriting fellowship at Brown University, where he assures me that racial dialogue happens very differently than it did in the Corps. But thinking back, he told me, "No one, including me, was offended. Everyone thought it was hilarious." The party continued, and the deployment followed without incident. The last Decaul heard of J. was recently, when he got a Facebook notification that J. wanted to "friend" him. "I turned him down," Maurice told me. "I thought, *I've had enough of you, J.*"

EVEN GIVEN THE youth of the Marines; the fact that the power structure of the unit had a significant number of black Americans; that America is more accepting of white radicalism than black radicalism; and that Marines are drawn like moths to a flame when it comes to the dangerous, the transgressive, and the darkly humorous, Decaul's claim that no one was offended is hard to accept. There are limits, after all, and they should probably stop well short of accommodating the most brutal domestic-terrorist organization in American history.

Sometimes Marines—not just white ones but also Marines of color—like to paint the military as a color-blind institution where people are judged for their abilities and character and not by their race or background. "The Marines don't have *any* race problems," General Daniel "Chappie" James Jr., the first black four-star general, is claimed to have said. "They treat everybody like they're black." This isn't true. The Americans who join the Corps bring with them the prejudices they inherited from American society. I heard some wild things in the military. Once, after going through the gas chamber, an exercise where Marines in training are exposed to CS gas, my whole unit was outside, tears streaming down our faces, long gobbets of snot hanging from our noses, our skin burning, when the sergeant instructor went up to one of us and said, "Hey, candidate! You're Jewish, right?" He pointed to the gas chamber and said, "You should go again. You're used to it." But whatever prejudices new Marines bring to the Corps also get filtered through a powerful group identity that changes the contours of how people interact and what their values are.

The most straightforward case of this was the fight over whether to permit gay people to serve in the military. Before the Don't Ask, Don't Tell policy was implemented, the Rand Corporation researched what effect allowing gays in the military would have on unit readiness. The argument against allowing gay people to serve was that the average soldier had such antipathy to gay men and women that it would hurt morale, limit the amount of good old homoeroticism that combat units run on, and generally make soldiers feel uncomfortable around one another in the intimate conditions that service in the military entails. But Rand's report, released in 1993, overwhelmingly concluded that this wouldn't be a problem. Not because Rand didn't find evidence of extreme homophobia in the military. I assure you, even a decade later, when I joined, such sentiments ran strong. The reason they didn't matter was because interpersonal attraction—the qualities someone has that, under normal circumstances, make you want to spend time with them outside of work—had no reliable impact on unit effectiveness. In fact, high social cohesion could even hurt unit effectiveness, by shifting individuals' priorities from the organizational to the social. Instead, the most important element was a shared commitment to a task. Emphasis on unity—rather than divisions along gender and race—as well as on the importance of the mission, was the crucial factor.

The reason it's a band of brothers, and not a band of friends, is because you can fight all day long with your brother and still be willing to die for him. J. wasn't the only misfit in Decaul's unit. Decaul's roommate was heavy into alcohol and hard drugs. "We used to get into fights all the time," Decaul told me. "I'm talking about fistfights." But the roommate's peers didn't get rid of him either, because out in the field the guy worked miracles on artillery pieces. The drug addict and the Klansman—both of whom should have been kicked out— were seen by their fellow Marines as contributing members of the unit, useful to the task at hand.

When a threat is existential, the qualities you value in an individual shift. Marines like Decaul weren't willing to work with a Klansman and a drug addict in spite of the fact that their lives might be on the line—they were willing to work with them *because* their lives were on the line. As the Corps saying goes, "You can trust a Marine with your life, but not your money or your wife."

The philosopher J. Glenn Gray, who served as an intelligence officer in World War II, marks this as the distinction between friendship and camaraderie. Friendship is a relationship between those who possess true emotional and intellectual affinity—they do not seek to lose their identity, but rather "find themselves in each other and thereby gain greater self-knowledge and self-possession." Camaraderie, by contrast, is about submersion in a collective. The Russian writer Vasily

Grossman, who covered the Battle of Stalingrad for the Red Army's newspaper, considered this submersion to be the crucial component of battlefield success. In battle, he wrote, "I am we, I am the mass of infantry going into the attack, I am the supporting tanks and artillery, I am the flare lighting up our common cause." Understanding how to manage this transition from the "frail, timid 'I'" to the "gallant, intelligent 'We'" was what Grossman considered "a key not only to the success of night-attacks by companies and battalions, but to the military success and failure of entire armies and peoples."

These feelings are temporary—Gray later noted the awkwardness of World War II–veteran reunions where the old fellow feeling could be reignited only with the strong application of effort and alcohol—but they're deeply powerful. For many people, they are the strongest and most intense feelings they'll experience in their life. How often do you look at a group of thirty men and women and think, *Any one of the people in this room might be called to die for me?*

Which means, when talking about making a military unit effective, we're not just talking about a grudging choice. We're talking about holding out the chance for that peculiar love born of camaraderie, a love that can exist between men who in normal circumstances would have no reason to love each other, men who might not even deserve such love. It is perhaps, as Martin Luther King Jr. said, a "brutal solidarity," but a solidarity nonetheless. That such a thing is even possible is in part thanks to the selfless character of the men and women who join the military, submit to the arduous training, and pledge to leave no one behind. But no less important is their commitment to something outside of the unit. They need a mission—one that is achievable, moral, and in keeping with the values of the society they represent and whose flag they wear on their uniform.

In the long term, the strength and legitimacy of the military will be a function of the perceived strength and legitimacy of the project it is supposed to represent. The clarity of purpose so central to bonding men in combat cannot emerge purely from the military itself. And in our current climate, after a decade and a half of multiple wars on multiple continents, the hope for such clarity is rotting away.

WHEN I LEFT the Corps, I was a firm believer in the mission, and I had cause to be. I had driven down Route Fran, past where Lonny Wells had died, past where many other Marines had died, or lost limbs, or had their face burned beyond recognition. Roadside bombs, sniper attacks, ambushes—Fran had been a regular site of death and violence. But my time on Fran didn't require much courage. I was there after Operation Alljah, which had cleared most of Fallujah's insurgents and set up joint security stations with the cooperation of the local tribes. As we were driving past piles of rubble, buildings riddled with bullet holes, and young Iraqi children riding bikes, we saw something we didn't expect. "Holy shit," one Marine said. "Is that . . . is that a bridal shop?"

And there it was, a newly opened bridal store, sitting on the edge of Fran. We couldn't believe it. "A bridal shop on Fran," another Marine said, sighing. "Jesus."

This was part of the much-heralded "success" of the surge, George W. Bush's decision to increase troop presence in Iraq and commit to a strategy grounded in the new counterinsurgency field manual General David Petraeus put out in 2006. Scholars and military strategists are still debating the degree to which the shift in policy helped cause that year's dramatic decline in violence, but for those of us on the ground, the connection was assumed.

Meanwhile, back home, a raucous debate about military policy was under way. When General Petraeus and Ryan Crocker, the ambassador to Iraq, came to testify before Congress in September 2007, the antiwar group MoveOn.org took out a full-page ad in *The New York Times* wondering whether Petraeus should be called "General Betray Us" and stating that he was "cooking the books for the White House." Hillary Clinton, then a senator from New York, told Petraeus and Crocker that it took "a willing suspension of disbelief" to accept their reports; House Speaker Nancy Pelosi declared that the plan they proposed sounded like "a ten-year, at least, commitment to an open-ended presence and war"; and when Republican senator John W. Warner asked whether the strategy in Iraq did anything to make America safer, he was told by Petraeus, "Sir, I don't know, actually." Two days later, President Bush gave a televised address to discuss what he saw as the progress in Iraq and to explain his rationale for a continued military commitment.

Hawks sometimes try to cast such debates as an affront to the troops. General John F. Kelly, a former Marine and the current White House chief of staff, once gave a speech in which he declared that service members "hold in disdain those who claim to support them but not the cause that takes their innocence, their limbs, and even their lives." But looking back, I realize that the cut and thrust of public debate were crucial in forming my own understanding of what our purpose was, and what success was supposed to look like. As a Marine in Iraq's Anbar Province in 2007, I could turn on the TV and see the various benchmarks of success in Iraq—security, political reconciliation, diplomatic engagement, economic and essential services—being debated in Congress. The Bush administration's claims were presented, attacked, defended, and presented again. The counterargument—that the gains of the surge were overstated and unlikely to achieve the broader political compromises essential for ensuring lasting stability in Iraq absent a large U.S. troop presence—received the same treatment.

The sheer heat of the arguments, for or against, made clear that the policy, and our presence, mattered.

I returned from Iraq in 2008, and within a year the Corps was ramping up for Afghanistan. When Barack Obama announced a surge of troops there, we felt like we were being called to repeat the Iraq "miracle," and suddenly Marines around me were angling to get on a deployment. Anbar was too safe, too boring. The fighting was in Afghanistan. And maybe lightning could strike twice. Maybe counterinsurgency theory really worked. At one point, I asked a young lance corporal out on a field exercise how his unit was going to be successful once they arrived in Helmand Province. I was expecting something along the lines of "By having a plan to kill everyone we meet." Instead, he told me they'd be successful "through cultural effectiveness, Sir," employing the language then being pushed down from his battalion commander, company commander, platoon commander, platoon sergeant, and squad leaders. It was a more hopeful time.

INSTEAD OF STAYING IN and hunting for a deployment, I chose to get out of the Corps and go to grad school. In my first year there, while settling into a comfortable life in New York, I found out that one Marine I had known, who'd volunteered for Afghanistan after I introduced him to a captain of a deploying unit, had died in the blast from a roadside bomb. I learned that a Marine I'd worked with closely had been hit by an improvised explosive device and taken shrapnel to his eyes that left him partially blind. I took a bus down to Walter Reed to see him, only to arrive hours after he'd been transferred to the West Coast. He recovered well, stayed in the Corps, is now a gunnery sergeant, and has a false eye with the Marine Corps' eagle, globe, and anchor emblem for a pupil.

Iraq was unraveling, and Afghanistan wasn't showing tremendous signs of progress. One Marine battalion fighting in Helmand Province in 2010 and 2011 suffered worse losses than any Marine battalion in the previous ten years of fighting. When asked by an embedded journalist what such sacrifices were for, the best that one of the sergeants in the battalion could muster was: "This war is stupid. Well, so what? Our country is in it."

An army friend of mine stationed in northern Afghanistan around this time wrote in a letter home, "There's no point in even imagining an end state for all of this because there isn't one—not through violence anyway." The next year, 2012, I received an email from a buddy who described the remoteness of where he'd been sent; the lack of the comforts he'd known when he was in Iraq, which had better chow and more reliable resupply; and how his biggest problem wasn't so much handling violence as "a maddeningly ambiguous environment with an ill-defined mission set they keep changing." Marines in Afghanistan started telling a joke about their enemy: "We have the watches," they'd say, "but they have the time."

Meanwhile, those Marines' elected leaders were doing everything they could to avoid the kind of public discussion that would have clarified the mission those men and women were carrying out. As special operators and advisers were reintroduced to Iraq, the Obama administration repeatedly insisted that those troops didn't count as "boots on the ground," leading some veterans to joke that special operators must wear combat slippers. In July 2015, President Obama bragged at a fundraiser, "We've ended two wars." No wonder our troops were having difficulty articulating why they were fighting. Their commander in chief couldn't even bring himself to admit that we were still at war.

The incoherence has deepened under President Trump. To ensure that victories against enemies like ISIS result in long-term stability and the suppression of new terrorist groups threatening our interests, the military has consistently articulated a vision of intergovernmental cooperation. That means cooperation among the Department of Defense, the intelligence community, the State Department, USAID, and other divisions that can provide humanitarian aid and development expertise. Former secretary of defense Robert M. Gates argued, "Without development we will not be successful in either Iraq or Afghanistan." Even former lieutenant general Michael Flynn, Trump's short-tenured national-security adviser, called at one point for a "Marshall Plan for the Middle East." But the Trump administration has shown little aptitude for or interest in such coordination and planning. In 2016, I had the opportunity to pose a question to then-candidate Trump at a televised veterans' forum. I asked him about his plan for *after* the fall of ISIS. He didn't have much of an answer, beyond the puzzling suggestion that we should "take the oil."

Unsurprisingly, then, the current military leadership has, if anything, been more assertive about the necessity of non-DOD support than they were during the Obama years. James Mattis—who as the commander of Centcom famously told Congress in 2013 that if it cut funding to the State Department, "I need to buy more ammunition"—has continued to advocate for the importance of diplomacy during his time as secretary of defense. General Joseph L. Votel, the current commander of Centcom, has said, "There is a lot that the military can do, but it is extraordinarily important that our diplomats, our Department of State, our other development agencies, and others are involved in this process as well," because if the United States doesn't integrate military objectives with soft-power capabilities, "we risk creating space for our adversaries to achieve their strategic aims."

Yet, in response to strong pressure from the DOD to fund nonlethal components of U.S. power, the Trump administration has proposed a 2019 budget that would cut State Department and USAID funding by 26 percent from the 2017 level and would cut the Treasury Department's international programs by 20 percent. Under former secretary of state Rex Tillerson's leadership, the State Department slowly bled close to 12 percent of its foreign-policy specialists; dozens of high-level positions remained unfilled; and retiring foreign-service officers told the press that morale has never been lower. In his speech last summer on Afghanistan policy, Donald Trump may have claimed that a "fundamental pillar of our new strategy is the integration of all instruments of American power—diplomatic, economic, and military— toward a successful outcome" and that "the brave defenders of the American people will have the necessary tools and rules of engagement to make this strategy work," but his administration has supplied few of the tools his own military leaders say are crucial to the mission.

Without a real integration of all instruments of American power, our recent military successes could potentially leave us no better off than we were after our military victory over al-Qaeda in Iraq. Believing the mission complete, the Obama administration followed those successes by limiting diplomatic engagement with Iraq, planning sharp cuts in civilian programs, and slashing economic assistance. A few years later the country was ripe for the rise of a new threat, which came in the form of ISIS. When we create a vacuum, something fills it. As Denise Natali, the director of the Center for Strategic Research, has pointed out, following the victory against ISIS in Mosul, militias backed by Iran's Islamic Revolutionary Guard Corps filled some of the void in services left by both Baghdad and the international community, and managed to recruit not only among Shia Muslims but even among Sunnis. In other words, simply by emphasizing the sort of soft power the current administration disdains, Iranian-backed militias are seeking to turn American and Iraqi tactical successes into Iranian strategic victories.

Meanwhile, the Trump administration has expanded lethal counterterrorism operations in Yemen, Pakistan, and Somalia—more than quintupling the number of such operations that had been performed during the final six months of the Obama presidency. But an onslaught of counterterror raids does not make a policy. As General Votel, who led Special Operations Command from 2014 to 2016, has noted, "We've been doing this long enough to know that leaders are killed, and we've killed plenty of them. And there's always somebody who is going to step up into those positions." People in the national-security community sometimes refer to these sorts of raids as "mowing the grass," which brings to mind the old infantryman's riddle, "What makes the grass grow?" The answer: blood.

One would think that almost seventeen years of war would have taught the American people and their elected leaders the limits of a strategy that focuses only on the use of military force without a broader endgame, but in fact we have moved in the opposite direction. Now we have a government that seeks to wage war without even the slightest interest in committing to precisely those efforts that our own military leaders insist are essential for victory. In June, Defense Secretary Mattis bluntly told Congress what the troops had known for years: "We are not winning in Afghanistan right now." Of course not. We don't want to win. We just want to take scalps.

"TOUGH LOVE in the Marine Corps. That's why I love the Corps so much. It's the only place I was ever loved. Tough love, but still."

Gunnery Sergeant Maxwell paced down the squad bay, with all of us young officer candidates standing at the position of attention, ready for inspection. This was 2004. The United States was fighting two wars—in Iraq and in Afghanistan. If we became Marine officers, we'd probably head to one or the other. Hopefully Iraq—Afghanistan didn't seem to have much going on. But first we had to get through Gunny Maxwell's inspection.

"You gotta deal with a lot of messed-up kids in the Marine Corps," he was saying. "They come from bad families, never got no love. Gotta give 'em tough love. That's why we're so hard on you."

Gunny Maxwell was huge. Memory always adds a few inches to the sergeant instructors who tormented you during Officer Candidates School, but he was definitely much taller than average. I'm six foot one, and as I stood at attention in front of Maxwell, my eyes didn't quite meet his chin.

More than his physicality, though, he had an intensity that seemed less put on, less of an act than most of the other sergeant instructors. Maxwell loved the Corps passionately. "The Marine Corps is the best doggone fighting force in the world," he told us once. "No—the best fighting force in the universe. Because if any doggone aliens come and try to mess with us, we'll fuck them up, too." He wanted us ready for conflict, whether our enemies were al-Qaeda, extraterrestrials, or "doggone pinko Red communist lefto Democrats."

Even to the lefto Democrats in the squad bay, this was an appealingly simple view: Just point us at the enemy. Sadly, the wars we'd end up fighting over the next decade and a half would be far murkier, and far more morally bruising, than your average Hollywood alien invasion. In June, the West Point graduate Fred Wellman went on Twitter to vent after having received what turned out to be a false report of a massacre in a small Iraqi town he'd visited in April 2003. He started by listing the people he'd worked with who had been touched by violence: an interpreter who'd been beheaded on video in 2004; a doctor who'd been blown up in 2006 and lost both his legs, only to return to work in the clinic Wellman had helped build, and who would be killed by militants there in 2011 after the withdrawal of U.S. forces. Then he wrote:

> At this point nearly every Iraqi I worked with over three tours has been murdered. . . . If someone knows a way I should process that I'm open to it but right now I'm just in shock at the brutality of war. I wish the leaders who claim to have balls because they send men like me to war actually felt the weight of dozens of deaths like me.

Later Wellman would learn the truth—instead of a massacre, four members of the Iraqi security forces had been killed. When it comes to a small town that spent time under occupation by ISIS, this is what counts as joyous news.

Wellman has nevertheless maintained a typically pragmatic, military approach to his service, which spanned twenty-two years, multiple wars, and presidents of both parties. When questioned recently by a Trump supporter as to why the Iraq War was worth the cost and loss of American life, Wellman responded, "As an old soldier I'm not one to be for or against the war I fought. I was ordered to go. I did it. My kid got orders. He went."

Is this enough to sustain a military—an iron sense of duty to a country unwilling to grapple seriously with the suffering caused by its mismanaged wars? Gunny Maxwell's certain projection of battlefield success has aged poorly in the intervening decade, and though our nation continues to produce men like Wellman, morale is hard to sustain when the burdens of war are shouldered by a few.

I've often heard veterans wish for a draft, for something that would drag more Americans into orbit around the dark star that is the country's constant exercise of military power. The founders of the republic originally wanted to force Congress to vote every two years just to keep a standing army; these days Congress won't even permit a vote to replace the Authorization for the Use of Military Force that was passed prior to the Iraq War and that we are now using to justify fighting against groups that didn't even exist back then.

For the military men and women overseas looking to explain why they're risking their lives, they have no public debate to refer to, no clear benchmarks of success being endlessly dissected and analyzed in Congress and on TV, as happened in 2007. Nor is there even clear guidance from the commander in chief, who one month rolls out an escalation in Afghanistan with the express purpose of increasing military pressure on the Taliban to motivate them to engage in a political settlement, and then a few months later announces that he's uninterested in negotiations and doesn't "see any talking taking place." Can service members maintain a sense of purpose when nobody—not the general public, or the Congress elected to represent them, or the commander in chief himself—seems to take the wars we're fighting seriously?

Our military is a major part of who we are as a country; it is the force that has undergirded the post–World War II international order. Being an American means being deeply implicated in that, for good or for ill. But as Wellman's response to his war suggests, the solution to our current dead end doesn't lie within the military itself. The military can't set its own goals, can't determine its own budget or which ideals it fights and dies for, and can't decide how its losses will be honored, dishonored, or appropriated after the fact. So while

America as a whole chooses to express its love for its military in gooey, substance-free displays, our military waits, perhaps hopelessly, for a coherent national policy that takes the country's wars seriously.

What would such a thing look like? It would probably look like rescinding the open-ended Authorization for the Use of Military Force and making the president regularly go before Congress to explain where and why he was putting troops in harm's way, what resources the mission required, and what the terms of success were. It would look like every member of Congress carrying out his or her constitutionally mandated duty to provide oversight of our military adventures by debating and then voting on that plan. It would look like average Americans taking part in that debate and scorning anyone who tried to tell them they couldn't. It would look like average Americans rolling their eyes in disgust when our leaders tell us we're not at war while American troops are risking their lives overseas, or when they claim that Americans must support the wars their country engages in if they want to support the troops, or when a press secretary argues that anyone who questions the success of a military raid in which a service member died "owes an apology" to that fallen soldier. It would look like our politicians letting the fallen rest in peace, rather than propping up their corpses for political cover. And when service members die overseas in unexpected places, such as the four killed in Niger last year, it would look like us eschewing the easy, symbolic debates about whether our president is disrespecting our troops by inartfully offering condolences or whether liberals are disrespecting our troops by seizing upon those inartful condolences for political gain. It would look like us instead having a longer and harder conversation about the mission we are asking soldiers to perform, and whether we are doing them the honor of making sure it's achievable.

In short, it would look like Americans as a whole doling out a lot fewer cheap, sentimental displays of love for our troops, and doubling down on something closer to Gunny Maxwell's "tough love"—a love that means zeroing in on our country's faults and failures.

IF WE DON'T, then at some point the bottom will drop out. Morale is a hard thing to measure, but plenty of indicators suggest that it's been falling. Ninety-one percent of troops called their quality of life good or excellent in a survey done by the *Military Times* back in 2009, when the downturn in violence in Iraq and a new strategy in Afghanistan still held out a promise of victory; by 2014 that had fallen to only 56 percent, with intentions to reenlist dropping from 72 to 63 percent. Recruiting is also down. For the past three decades, the military has generally accepted about 60 percent of applicants. In recent years that figure has been closer to 70 percent and is climbing. And the active-duty force is getting worn out. When I was in, I was impressed to meet guys with five deployments under their belts. Now I meet guys who have done eight, or nine, or ten. The situation is particularly bad within the Special Operations community. Last year Special Operations Command deployed troops to 149 countries; some operators cycled in and out of deployments at what General Raymond Thomas called the "unsustainable" pace of six months overseas, six months at home. I recently met an Army Ranger who'd done seven deployments. He was on a stateside duty and told me that when he and his wife realized that he'd be home for two years straight, it freaked them out a bit. They loved each other and had three kids but had never spent two solid years together without one of them going on a deployment. This is too much to ask, especially for ongoing wars with no end in sight.

Theresa Whelan, the principal deputy assistant secretary of defense for homeland defense and global security, recently told the House Armed Services Committee that the Special Operations community has "had to eat our young . . . [and] mortgaged our future" to keep going.

Day by day, that mortgaged future creeps closer. When it arrives, who is going to sign up for a vague and hopeless mission? How do you motivate men and women to fight and die for a cause many of them don't believe in, and whose purpose they can't articulate? What happens to the bonds between men and women in combat, and to the bonds between soldiers and the citizenry for whom they fight, when we fail as a nation to treat our wars as a collective responsibility rather than the special mission of a self-selected few?

Without a political leadership that articulates and argues for a mission and objective worth dying for, it's no surprise that soldiers sometimes stop caring about the mission altogether. A sergeant who deployed to the Korengal Valley, in Afghanistan, told me that by the end of his deployment, he had purposely adopted a defensive posture, sacrificing mission for safety at every opportunity he could. This is reminiscent of what one officer said of the later stages of the Vietnam War: "The gung-ho attitude that made our soldiers so effective in 1966, '67, was replaced by the will to survive." It's not that those troops lacked courage, but that the ends shifted. "We fought for each other," I've heard plenty of veterans claim about their time in service, and no wonder. If your country won't even resource the wars with what its own generals say is necessary for long-term success, what else is there to fight for? But if you think the mission your country keeps sending you on is pointless or impossible and that you're only deploying to protect your brothers and sisters in arms from danger, then it's not the Taliban or al-Qaeda or ISIS that's trying to kill you, it's America.

WHAT WE'RE FIGHTING FOR

FEBRUARY 10, 2017

When his convoy was ambushed during the 2003 invasion of Iraq, First Lieutenant Brian Chontosh ordered his Humvee driver to head straight into the oncoming machine-gun fire. They punched through, landing in a trench full of heavily armed Iraqi soldiers. Lieutenant Chontosh and his Marines leapt out and he ran down the trench firing away, dropping one enemy soldier after another. First his rifle jammed, then he ran out of ammunition, so he switched to his pistol. He shot it dry, reloaded, and shot it dry again. So he picked up an AK-47 from a dead Iraqi, fired that dry, picked up another AK, fired that dry, picked up a rocket-propelled grenade, fired it, and led the group back to the Humvee, their attack having almost completely cleared the trench. Almost.

One Iraqi was playing dead, fiddling with the pin of a grenade. Lieutenant Chontosh had no ammo, but on the ground were a couple of M16 rounds from when his rifle had jammed. He grabbed one, loaded, and before the Iraqi could pull the pin, Lieutenant Chontosh locked eyes with him and shot him dead. All told, according to the journalist Phil Zabriskie's account of the ambush in "The Kill Switch," Lieutenant Chontosh had killed about two dozen people that day.

When I was a new Marine, just entering the Corps, this story from the Iraq invasion defined heroism for me. It's a perfect image of war for inspiring new officer candidates, right in line with youthful notions of what war is and what kind of courage it takes—physical courage, full stop. We thought it was a shame more Americans didn't know the story.

But after spending thirteen months in Iraq, after seeing violence go down not because we managed to increase our lethality but because we improved our ability to work with Iraqis, I became convinced that there were other stories of war equally important for Americans to understand. And as we look at a president who claims that he wants to "fight fire with fire" in the battle against jihadism, I think back to the stories that defined, for me, what it meant to be an American at war, and the reasons I was proud to wear the uniform.

I was sent to Iraq in January 2007 with a logistics unit, the sort unlikely to engage in Chontosh-style heroics. We managed the key parts of an army people often forget about: truck drivers, engineers, explosive disposal specialists, postal workers—and, crucially, doctors.

Midway through my deployment, a Marine arrived on base with severe wounds. He'd been shot by an enemy sniper, and the medical staff swarmed around his body, working frantically, skillfully, but it wasn't enough. He died on the table.

Normally, there'd be a moment of silence, of prayer, but the team got word that the man who killed this young Marine, the insurgent sniper, would be arriving a few minutes later. That dead Marine's squadmates had engaged the sniper in a firefight, shot him a couple of times, patched him up, bandaged him, and called for a casualty evacuation to save the life of the man who'd killed their friend.

So he arrived at our base. And the medical staff members, still absorbing the blow of losing a Marine, got to work. They stabilized their enemy and pumped him full of American blood, donated from the "walking blood bank" of nearby Marines. The sniper lived. And then they put him on a helicopter to go to a hospital for follow-up care, and one of the navy nurses was assigned to be his flight nurse. He told me later of the strangeness of sitting in the back of a helicopter, watching over his enemy lying peacefully unconscious, doped up on painkillers, while he kept checking the sniper's vitals, his blood pressure, his heartbeat, a heartbeat that was steady and strong thanks to the gift of blood from the Americans this insurgent would have liked to kill.

This wasn't just a couple of Marines and sailors making the right decision. These weren't acts of exceptional moral courage in the way Lieutenant Chontosh's acts were acts of exceptional physical courage. This was standard policy, part of tradition stretching back to the Revolutionary War, when George Washington ordered every soldier in the Continental Army to sign a copy of rules intended to limit harm to civilians and ensure that their conduct respected what he called "the rights of humanity," so that their restraint "justly secured to us the attachment of all good men."

From our founding we have made these kinds of moral demands of our soldiers. It starts with the oath they swear to support and defend the Constitution, an oath made not to a flag, or to a piece of ground, or to an ethnically distinct people, but to a set of principles established in our founding documents. An oath that demands a commitment to democracy, to liberty, to the rule of law, and to the self-evident equality of all men. The Marines I knew fought, and some of them died, for these principles.

That's why those Marines were trained to care for their enemy. That's why another Marine gave his own blood to an insurgent. Because America is an idea as much as a country, and so those acts defend America as surely as any act of violence, because they embody that idea. That nurse, in the quiet, alone with that insurgent, with no one looking as he cared for his patient. That was an act of war.

After I left the Marine Corps, I met a veteran named Eric Fair. He was quiet. He wrote strange and affecting stories about guilt and alienation, and at first he didn't tell me much about his past. Only over time did I learn that he'd been an army Arabic linguist before September 11, and then had signed up as a contractor and gone to Abu Ghraib prison in January 2004, all things he would later write about in his memoir, *Consequence*.

Back then Abu Ghraib was a mess, he told me. Thousands of Iraqis, some of them insurgents, plenty of them innocent civilians caught up in the postinvasion chaos, and far too few qualified interrogators to sort it out. And the information they were seeking—it was literally life or death.

So Eric began crossing lines. Not legal lines—he followed the rules. But moral lines, personal lines, lines where it was clear that he wasn't treating the people in his interrogation booth like human beings.

One time, it was with a boy captured with car batteries and electronic devices. The boy said his father used the batteries for fishing, an explanation that Eric found absurd. So he used the approved techniques. Light slaps, stress positions. The boy eventually broke and, weeping, told Eric about a shop where his father delivered the electronics.

When a unit was sent to raid the shop, it found half a dozen partly assembled car bombs. "It was an enormous adrenaline rush," he told me. He'd used techniques he now considers torture and, he thought, saved lives.

So, naturally, he kept using them. There were a large number of detainees caught with car batteries, all of them with the same story about fishing. With them, Eric would go right to the techniques designed to humiliate, to degrade, to make people suffer until they tell you what you want to hear. But Eric didn't get any more results. No more car bomb factories. Just a lot of broken, weeping detainees.

Eventually, he told a fellow contractor the ridiculous fishing story, and how he wasn't falling for it, and the contractor told him: "Of course they fish with car batteries. I used to do it in Georgia." The electric charge stuns the fish, a simple method for an easy meal.

Eric isn't sure how many innocent Iraqis he hurt. All he knows is how easy it was for him to cross the line. Just as for the nurse with that wounded insurgent there was a codified set of procedures in place to help guide Marines and navy medical personnel to make moral choices, choices they could tell their children and grandchildren about without shame, for Eric there was a codified set of procedures beckoning him to take actions that he now feels condemn him.

He doesn't even have the consolation of feeling that he saved lives. Sure, they found a car bomb factory, but Abu Ghraib was a turning point. In 2003, thousands of Iraqi soldiers had begun surrendering to the United States, confident they'd be treated well. That's thousands of soldiers we didn't have to fight to the death because of the moral reputation of our country.

Abu Ghraib changed things. Insurgent attacks increased, support for the sectarian leader Muqtada al-Sadr surged, and 92 percent of Iraqis claimed they saw coalition forces as occupiers rather than liberators or peacekeepers. WikiLeaks later released a United States assessment that detainee mistreatment at Abu Ghraib and Guantánamo was "the single most important motivating factor" convincing foreign jihadists to wage war, and General Stanley McChrystal said, "In my experience, we found that nearly every first-time jihadist claimed Abu Ghraib had first jolted him to action." Our moral reputation had started killing American soldiers.

So, yeah, they found a car bomb factory. Once.

Eric has a relationship to his war that's much different from mine. Yet we were in the same war. And Eric did what our nation asked of him, used techniques that were vetted and approved and passed down to intelligence operatives and contractors like himself. Lawyers at the highest levels of government had been consulted, asked to bring us to the furthest edge of what the law might allow. To do what it takes, regardless of whether such actions will secure the "attachment of all good men" or live up to that oath we swear to support and defend the Constitution.

What to make of that oath, anyway? The Constitution seems to mean different things at different times and places—whether in my unit's dusty little combat hospital, or in Eric's interrogation booth, or in a stadium where a crowd cheers a presidential candidate vowing to torture his nation's enemies. We live in a democracy, so that document can be bent and twisted and re-formed to mean whatever we want it to.

If we choose to believe in a morally diminished America, an America that pursues its narrow, selfish interests and no more, we can take that course and see how far it gets us. But if we choose to believe that America is not just a set of borders, but a set of principles, we need to act accordingly. That is the only way we ensure that our founding document, and the principles embedded within, are alive enough, and honorable enough, to be worth fighting for.

Which brings me back to Brian Chontosh, that man with such

incredible skill at killing for his country. Years after I left the Corps, I was surprised to learn that he didn't really put much stock in his exceptional kill count. He told Phil Zabriskie this about killing: "It's ugly, it's violent, it's disgusting. I wish it wasn't part of what we had to do."

When people ask him if he's proud of what he did, he answers: "I'm not proud of killing a whole lot of people. That doesn't make sense to me. I'm proud of who I am today because I think I've done well. I think I've been honorable. I've been successful for my men, for the cause, for what's right."

Brian Chontosh doesn't dwell on the dead, but he does wonder whether there were times when, perhaps, he need not have killed. One of these is that last soldier in the trench. He'll remember him, trying to pretend he's dead but wiggling a bit. "It's not a haunting image," he told Zabriskie. "It's just—man. I wonder. I wonder if I would have just freaking grabbed the dude. Grabbed his hand, thrown the grenade away or something. I could have got him some medical treatment."

If he had, then that enemy soldier would have ended up with a unit like mine, surrounded by doctors and nurses and navy corpsmen who would have cared for him in accordance with the rule of law. They would have treated him well, because they're American soldiers, because they swore an oath, because they have principles, because they have honor. And because without that, there's nothing worth fighting for.

FEAR AND LOATHING IN MOSUL

SPRING 2020

This past December I stood on a rooftop in the center of the ancient Nabi Jarjis neighborhood in Mosul. Coalition bombing runs during the October 2016 to July 2017 battle to retake the city from ISIS had left large sections of the area leveled. The home I stood on had only recently been reconstructed by the United Nations Development Program, which is rebuilding fifteen thousand homes in the area. In the utterly shattered building next door, I could make out Ottoman-era brickwork exposed by the bombing. Nearby, the remains of an eleventh-century mosque. Across the river, the site of a destroyed seventh-century mosque beneath which ISIS fighters (of all people) had dug tunnels and discovered Assyrian artwork from the seventh century B.C. To walk through the city was to come into physical contact with centuries and millennia past, exposed not by careful archaeological work, but by the blunt instruments of war.

Later that night, my appreciation of this complex layering of past and present deepened as I reread *They Will Have to Die Now*, reporter James Verini's superb account of Mosul and the fall of the Islamic State's caliphate. Verini covered the brutal battle to retake the city with almost suicidal courage. He could easily have written a book anchored in the tactical advances of the army, letting us observe one neighborhood falling after the next, chronologically, until it all ends in a sorrowful but narratively satisfying victory amid the ruins of the ancient city. But that kind of neat beginning, middle, and end would be false. At this point, in Iraq any war narrative with a neat beginning, middle, and end is a lie. Thus Verini gives an account not simply of the battle—of the complex interplay of political factions, ethnic and religious groupings, military technology, foreign influence, and the sheer weight of violence and trauma—but also of the historical fault lines that are the true narrative of this war, peeking up from below.

Mosul's history goes back at least six thousand years, a fortress city (*muswila,* one of its earliest names, literally means "western fortress") later raised to prominence as a temple city of the Assyrians. Verini makes much of that mixture of military and religious purpose marking the city, and his account of the Assyrian kings is concerned less with the rise and fall of empire than with the way war-making figured as a sacred obligation. "I made their gullets and entrails run down upon the wide earth," brags a typical cuneiform inscription from an Assyrian king. "My prancing steeds harnessed for my riding, I plunged into the streams of their blood as into a river." In the Assyrian worldview, "the state was also the cosmos, the realm of holy order. Outside was chaos, unformed, unholy . . . it was the responsibility of the Assyrian king to carry on the work of creation, to perpetuate the order the gods had introduced at time's beginning. He did this through combat."

THE RISE AND FALL OF THE ISLAMIC STATE

One of the pleasures of Verini's book is watching how he takes this notion, at first presented as an exotic and atavistic grotesquery, and traces its changing forms to the present day. We hear echoes of Assyrian kings not only when we learn of Saddam Hussein embracing an Islamic-inflected postcolonial nationalism and commissioning a Koran written in his own blood, but also when we learn of the British Royal Air Force's insistence, during its cruel 1920s campaign in Iraq, that "bombing from the air is regarded almost as an act of God to which there is no effective reply but immediate submission." Verini takes us from ancient Assyrian carvings to medieval Islamic wars, from Mosul's biblical cameos to the 1919 Paris Peace Conference, with sacralized violence always somewhere in the background.

The American invasion of Iraq, though, sparked an obsessive and paranoid style in jihadism that brought this religiously inflected view of violence and state-building to its peak. Traditional religious authorities, unable to cope with the apocalyptic image of a hostile world overrun with infidel forces, were overturned. Jihadis like Abu Musab al-Zarqawi, the founder of ISIS, promoted a revolutionary and highly individualistic version of Islam, a turn Verini posits as akin to a hyperviolent Protestant Reformation. "Next to faith, there is nothing more important than repulsing an assailant enemy who ruins the religion and the world," Zarqawi wrote in "Our Creed and Methodology." "There is no condition to jihad." As our seemingly jealous president once complained, "We are playing by the rules, but they have no rules."

Intriguingly, though, in Mosul, the group initially modulated its violence in a bid for public support. Readers used to the West's often lurid and shallow news coverage of ISIS (coverage Verini accuses of existing "somewhere on the same spectrum as the Caliphate's own blood-porn") might be surprised to learn that when ISIS took the city of Mosul in 2014, life got better—especially if you were a Sunni, preferably male. Nevertheless, ISIS started with a soft approach. They hired garbage collectors, lowered rents, fixed sewers, opened markets, tried to cut down on corruption. "People thought it was a revolution," a Moslawi told me this December. "Many people joined Daesh in those months," he said, using a common term for ISIS, "but then reality came, and there were only two ways out. Either you die fighting, or Daesh kills you."

Of course there was brutality in those initial days, too. But from a certain perspective, the brutality seemed a wash. Early on in *They Will Have to Die Now*, Verini tells the story of Abu Fahad, whose extended family is a recurring thread throughout the book and a window into life in Mosul before the battle and after. Abu Fahad, a nurse and pharmacist, is an educated and eloquent man who'd prefer to leave Mosul behind and live in America. His daughter speaks openly of politics and religion, loves Ryan Reynolds, admires Hillary Clinton, and thinks Donald Trump is a hateful buffoon. Verini asks them about life under ISIS and is shown a video of a mentally disabled boy who'd defied curfew and was shot by a sniper, his corpse left outside for days. But then Abu Fahad switches to a story from 2006, and he describes what happened when he drove with his wife toward a checkpoint manned by Kurdish and American soldiers: bullets crashed through the window; he was dragged from the vehicle and beaten unconscious. When he came to, he found his wife's corpse. And when he reached his eldest daughter, who had seen her mother's head explode, she was sitting in the back seat, trying to eat glass. "We were one of the families who welcomed Daesh," he told Verini, looking him in the eye, without a hint of abashment.

Systems of order based on violence, though, have a tendency to devour themselves in the chaos they create. Whereas the Americans and British players in Mosul's history sometimes delude themselves into thinking that the application of savagery can create a stable order, ISIS always understood itself as an apocalyptic organization, its violence a means of rushing forward to the end-times. "Much more than homicidal," Verini tells us, "the Islamic State was suicidal."

And so, ISIS's brutality would eventually eliminate the initial sympathy it had earned. An early turning point was the 2014 Speicher Massacre, in which ISIS captured a large group of Iraqi Air Force cadets, brought them to an old Saddam palace, and murdered the fifteen hundred mostly Shia young men one by one. It was an Abu Ghraib–style self-inflicted wound. Until then, ISIS had support from many moderate Sunnis, people Verini insists "you and I would consider sane and sympathetic. . . . Sunnis who looked at the wider Sunni stage— the selfish monarchies of the Gulf; the brutal, secularist military of Egypt, which had deposed and imprisoned the legitimately elected Muslim Brotherhood; the imperious Turks; Iran-dominated Lebanon— and saw a void of valid leadership." The Speicher Massacre exposed ISIS as the death cult it was, and not the hoped-for Sunni answer to the Iranian revolution.

From there on, ISIS had begun losing the moral battle. What was left was the slow and cruel physical battle, which Verini details from a frontline perspective. It comes in fragments, a series of vignettes from his reporting—sketches of the culture of Iraqi Special Forces, a profile of an Iraqi general, of ISIS's marketing genius, Iraqi attitudes toward the United States, life in the refugee camps for fleeing Moslawis, and so on. The method is fragmentary because Iraqi politics and society are fragmented. Mosul was the apogee of this, with historic Sunni and Shia and Yazidi and Christian and Kurdish communities coexisting.

Moslawis will tell you that Mosul is a microcosm of all Iraq, which is why, as the fragments intersect with the history that Verini provides to contextualize them, you come to understand the reason one of his sources, a refugee from the battle, would claim, "Mosul's history was essential to Iraq's history—and to the world's."

Verini has a jaunty, ironic style, a great eye for details, and an ear for telling quotes. We see "the sheer mystical velocity of twenty-first-century mechanized-digitized combat" coordinated over a WhatsApp channel, and learn the Kurdish peshmerga is "more an attitude than an army." He describes ISIS's how-to videos for suicide car bombs as like "very sinister episodes of the old MTV show *Pimp My Ride*," and the liberties Shia militiamen took with their battle dress "as though they'd been kitted out at some urban unisex martial athleisure boutique." At one point, he follows a student through the recently liberated rubble of Mosul University. Looking out upon what remains, the student declares, "I don't see the reason we're not back here studying. . . . There's everything. There's chairs."

At times, Verini drops single paragraphs that serve as parables of the war, like one about an Iraqi major trained as an attorney. He wanted to practice human rights law after the war but in the meantime had a policy of executing suspected ISIS captives because "it's true we have human rights here . . . but Daesh doesn't deserve anything like that." The paragraph ends, "I offered no rejoinder to the major. He was killed by an IED not long after."

More than anything, Verini captures the disorienting weirdness of war. "Experientially, war is mostly sound," he tells us. It is only afterward that journalists and filmmakers compose it into visually coherent scenes. In the moment, you listen to bombs, rockets, and gunfire all day and night, rarely seeing them impact or even leave a muzzle, mostly bored. Meanwhile, Iraqi soldiers and Kurdish peshmerga with cell phones take selfies, talk to their mothers in between firefights, and argue about who is having sex with whose sister, all while the American military calls in air strikes on houses they pretend not to know have civilians inside.

THE FORGOTTEN FOREVER WARS

Verini has provided us, at great physical risk and with impressive intellectual rigor, a map of the complex factors that determined—and still determine—our success or failure against groups like ISIS in Iraq. There is a question, though, that I felt haunted by as I read and reread *They Will Have to Die Now.* Put bluntly: Does it matter? After all, for me the most surprising bit of the book was not any revelation about ISIS or Iraqi history, but a simple statement Verini makes toward the beginning about his motivations for heading there in the first place, after almost a decade and a half of avoiding the war as a journalist: "I had to write about this country whose story had been entwined with my country's story for a generation now, for most of my life, so entwined that neither place any longer made sense without the other." And more to the point, he asks, "As an American writer of my age, how do you not face Iraq?"

But of course, in a war-weary America, where that weariness touches the writing community as well, it's quite easy to not face Iraq. Quality books about the wars often seem overlooked, missing from award long lists, relegated to niche discussions. This November, when *Slate* compiled its list of the fifty greatest nonfiction books of the past twenty-five years, it didn't include a single title dealing with either Iraq or Afghanistan, wars that have defined so much of the past two decades and produced writing of the highest order, from writers like

Dexter Filkins, Anand Gopal, Emma Sky, Elliot Ackerman, Elizabeth Samet, C. J. Chivers, and Anthony Shadid. Indeed, the tone one sometimes encounters is best summed up by a recent *New Yorker* review of an art show featuring contemporary artists, including thirty-six Iraqis and Kuwaitis, dealing with the Gulf Wars. It began, "I have rarely looked forward with less appetite to any art show than I did to 'Theater of Operations: The Gulf Wars, 1991–2011,'" and before panning the show, the reviewer, Peter Schjeldahl, went on to ask his readers, "Why revisit the concatenating disasters in Iraq for which my nation bears responsibility" and "whose terrible consequences have not ceased since Barack Obama declared an end to American combat involvement in 2010?"

Let us set aside, for the moment, that a grown man who is paid to think thoughts and write about them in one of America's premier magazines seems to be under the impression that American combat involvement in Iraq actually ended in 2010. The sentence provoked rage among many of the war writers I know, but at least it had a certain honesty to it, reminiscent of when W. B. Yeats contemptuously dismissed the English trench poets of World War I by declaring "passive suffering is not a theme for poetry."

In the days before reading that review, I'd gone to western Mosul, where shattered houses and omnipresent rubble call to mind old World War II photos of the aftermath of Allied campaigns, and where the residents rebuild amid ruins that are still full of bodies, killed by American bombs dropped over a half decade after Obama's declaration. Earlier, in Sinjar, I met with Yazidi survivors of ISIS's genocide, and with members of a group seeking to liberate the Yazidi women still held in captivity. One of them asked, "Why are we not having enough attention from your side? We have high numbers of survivors, people in mass graves, why don't we have assistance?"

The first thought that occurred to me, reflecting on Mr. Schjeldahl's sentence, was that the Yazidi operation didn't have enough attention because, at this stage of the war, their suffering was no longer aesthetically interesting to Americans. Nor—after both Republican and Democratic presidents had bloodied their hands and where much of our involvement is handled with minimal troop presence and even less fanfare—was it politically interesting. Passive suffering is not a theme for poetry.

All this assumes, of course, that "passive suffering" is an apt description of what's going on in Iraq. But Iraqis, as Verini points out, "have a genius for putting things behind them . . . metabolizing misfortune down to near simultaneity." In Mosul today, the massive task of rebuilding continues, often hand in hand with partially U.S.-funded international organizations that—having learned some lessons from the long history of development failures in Iraq—target their aid hyperlocally rather than allowing it to be filtered through corrupt or sectarian institutions (a significant exception to this being America's sectarian support for the Iraqi Christian community, which has stoked some tensions).

Thus, the UNHCR runs camps for those displaced by violence, operates a community center and safe house in Sinjar for women who'd been enslaved by ISIS, provides aid at the community and village level to restore water and electric services, and in some cases provides cash-based assistance tracked with biometrics. The UNDP, when rebuilding homes, works with local Moslawi contractors directly. The U.S. Institute of Peace partners with local ethnic and religious leaders to enable the safe return of the displaced, prevent postreturn violence, and help local communities participate in district and subdistrict budgeting.

Are such efforts enough? Iraq's central government is weak, corrupt, sectarian, dysfunctional, and currently wracked by ongoing protests. The governor of Ninevah Province, where Mosul is located, says it will take another decade and at least $15 billion to restore the city to its pre-ISIS state. Moslawis say ISIS could never return to the city after what they'd put the people through, but ISIS cells remain active in the rural areas, and tens of thousands of "ISIS-affiliated" families ("affiliation" meaning up to as much as five degrees of separation from an ISIS member) still languish in camps. The majority of those in camps are children, vulnerable to radicalization and with little chance of being reintegrated back into society anytime soon. Sectarian militias are everywhere, often treating the populations in a predatory, abusive, or deadly manner.

Meanwhile, America continues to withdraw nonmilitary support to the country. In December, the State Department sent plans to Congress to reduce staff at its embassy and consulate by 28 percent. This will thin an already reduced mission, in which diplomats have far less presence than before and where excessively defensive post-Benghazi security protocols mean that even in relatively safe cities, like Erbil, diplomats live in a disconnected bubble, unable to walk even half a block from their consulate and have a coffee in the nearby Hard Rock Cafe. Five thousand troops, of course, remain. We may have "defeated" ISIS, but the conditions that bred them persist, and we have less interest than ever before in trying to manage those conditions with anything other than violence.

THE NEXT CHAPTER

As I write this, the United States is preparing to send more troops to the Middle East, expecting further retaliation (in addition to the largely symbolic January 8 ballistic missile strikes against two Iraqi military bases housing U.S. troops) for our January 3 airstrike near the Baghdad airport that killed Major General Qassim Suleimani, the powerful head of Iran's Islamic Revolutionary Guard Corps's Quds Force, along with Abu Mahdi al-Muhandis, a commander of an umbrella group of Iranian-backed militias in Iraq. The killing followed a series of escalations between Iran and the United States, starting with rocket attacks on an Iraqi military base that killed an American contractor, followed by U.S. airstrikes on an Iranian-backed Iraqi militia, killing twenty-four and wounding fifty, followed by a militia-led siege of the U.S. embassy in Baghdad.

Iraq had already been in turmoil; months of widespread protests had forced the prime minister to resign. The protests, which have been anticorruption, antisectarian, and opposed to foreign influence in Iraq, had for the most part focused their anger not against the United States, but against Iran, at one point even burning an Iranian consulate. And though Suleimani was hated by many of the protesters (Iranian-backed militias were responsible for killing hundreds of peacefully demonstrating Iraqis in the previous months), within hours of the strike the Iraqi prime minister released a statement calling the killings "a flagrant violation of Iraqi sovereignty" and announced that the Iraqi Parliament would begin considering measures to "preserve the dignity of Iraq and its security and sovereignty." Undoubtedly, this strengthens the hand of Iran's allies, who seek to limit U.S. influence. Almost certainly, there will be more violence, the brunt of it born by Iraqis caught in a conflict they didn't choose. And it may effectively end the push for government reforms as Iraq falls further back into crisis.

Where does it all end? In the wake of the strike, our secretary of defense declared the attack was aimed at deterring future attacks, and our secretary of state declared, "We have every expectation that people not only in Iraq, but in Iran, will view the American action last night as giving them freedom." But such promises have been made before. And the Trump administration is hardly the first American administration to substitute targeted killing for a strategy. Meanwhile, a former interpreter for U.S. forces living in Baghdad asks me to pray for him and his family's safety.

Even now, despite the past two decades, and despite the veritable library of books like Verini's telling us otherwise, Americans still elect administrations that treat Iraq like a blank slate, without history or context or national pride, and that will respond to our actions only as we wish. Which is a roundabout way of saying that yes, books like Verini's very much matter, or at least should—especially if we're going to be involved, for the foreseeable future, in a country where history old and new lives as vibrantly as it does in Iraq.

The last site I visited in the old city of Mosul was the ruins of the al-Nuri Grand Mosque. Built in the twelfth century, the mosque was a symbol of Mosul. ISIS destroyed it in 2017. The other Americans and I walked through the rubble, past the stones of its famous minaret scattered by explosives, our eyes on the devastation. A normally garrulous and unflappable foreign policy analyst turned to a Moslawi woman. "I'm speechless," he said.

She stared out at the UNDP workers categorizing the seven bands of stone that had made up the minaret, preparing them to be reassembled. "I'm happy," she replied, "because I see they have started rehabilitation."

WE HAVE NO IDEA WHAT WE'RE DOING IN IRAQ. WE DIDN'T BEFORE WE KILLED SULEIMANI.

JANUARY 9, 2020

I was in Iraq's Anbar Province in 2007 during Operation Alljah, when the Marines pushed the insurgency out of Fallujah. The second time. The first time was in 2004; back then, America lost eighty-two Marines and soldiers taking the city. Suffered six hundred wounded. Both times, we were (briefly) victorious. By 2016, we were taking back the city once more, this time from the Islamic State. Yet again, a victory.

Perhaps the new decade will bring new battles for the same turf. If so, I'm sure we'll win the fourth or even fifth time. We're America. We're good at violence. At fighting hard. Expelling insurgents from cities in Iraq or districts in Afghanistan. But we're not good at making sure the violence leads to long-term stability.

That's why I found it hard to welcome the recent airstrike in Iraq that killed Qassim Suleimani, the Iranian Quds Force commander, despite all the blood on his hands. Violence is a destabilizing tool, Iraq is a volatile country, and when I ask myself how this strike might contribute to our long-term goals in the region, I have difficulty coming up with good answers. Watching President Trump's speech Wednesday morning in response to Iran's retaliatory missiles fired at U.S. troops in Iraq, wherein he bragged about our military capabilities but barely mentioned the situation on the ground, didn't clarify much.

In theory, our presence there now, seventeen years after the Iraq War began, is primarily about countering the Islamic State (which joined the insurgency against the U.S. occupation in 2004, about a year after President George W. Bush declared that our first mission there was accomplished). When Donald Trump was campaigning against Hillary Clinton in 2016, he even claimed to have a "secret plan" to defeat the group. But I'd seen insurgent groups "defeated" before, and so when I had a chance, at NBC's 2016 "Commander-in-Chief Forum," to ask Trump a question, I didn't ask about that plan. I asked what would happen next, after he sent troops to bleed and die and kill, securing towns and villages overseas. What would he do to ensure that the insurgents didn't just come back? He gave a rambling answer, criticizing Barack Obama's pullout from Iraq and blaming it for the Islamic State's rise, before declaring we should have "taken the oil."

In the years since, Trump's strategic thinking doesn't seem to have advanced much. The Islamic State has been stripped of its territory; Trump's "secret plan" turned out to be continuing Obama's policy of airstrikes and deployments of Special Operations troops in support of local forces, and from a purely military perspective it may have worked. But the situation remains fragile. Even before the airstrike that killed Suleimani, Iraq was in a dangerous state of flux. Massive protests demanding wide-ranging reforms challenged the political class, a refugee crisis strained resources, and sectarian militias intimidated, harassed, or killed civilians. Last month, while I was on a trip there, Iraqi officials, former Iraqi military commanders, international aid workers, and small-town mayors all repeated the same worry to me: that without further stabilization efforts to allow people to return home, the camps for displaced people would become incubators for new insurgencies.

Then there are the cross-border problems. In a refugee camp in northern Iraq, I met a Syrian who'd been injured in a rocket strike after Trump withdrew U.S. forces from northern Syria and allowed Turkey to invade; he told me, "There was security when the U.S. was in Syria, but the U.S. betrayed us." He had six metal pins sticking out of his leg, from upper thigh to knee, and was living in a tent with his pregnant wife and two children, awaiting the deepening winter with trepidation. His people, the Kurds, had fought with Americans against the Islamic State, only to watch us turn our backs on them. But, he warned, "ISIS will come back." If that's true, the Obama-Trump policy, reliant on local allies, will be a harder sell.

And so once again, having spent blood and treasure achieving tactical successes in the Middle East, we are faced with the question of how we might secure some strategic benefit. Or at the very least prevent a relapse into utter chaos. And the Trump administration's answer seems to be erratic violence inflicted across the region.

The current cycle of escalation between the United States and Iran, with Iraq as the battlefield, suggests the limits of this approach. The Iraqi prime minister declared the recent airstrikes a "flagrant violation of Iraqi sovereignty," the parliament voted 170–0 in favor of expelling U.S. troops from the country, and NATO forces working with Iraqi soldiers fighting the Islamic State began exiting. Adding to the mess, the U.S. military accidentally released a draft memo incorrectly stating that American troops were preparing to leave, too. Trump did insist in his Wednesday speech that he wanted to work with the Iranians on the mission against the Islamic State, the only thing in Iraq our president claimed to care about (aside from oil) when he was campaigning. But recent events have put that mission in jeopardy.

Watching our Iraq maneuvers unfold, it seems clear that, more than three years after I asked Trump how he might avoid repeating what he considered Obama's failures in Iraq, the president still has no clear answer. It's a terrible thing, having no rational foreign policy in a volatile region where you are regularly killing people. Nevertheless, as the military prepares to send more troops to the Middle East, I wonder if Obama could honestly have answered my question much better. After all, though our previous president was less erratic than this one, Obama's Middle East policy was hardly the epitome of coherence—withdrawing and then quietly ramping up military support to Iraq, proclaiming the virtues of American soft power while slashing nonmilitary assistance, all the while evading discussion of the war and its costs.

At an event in May 2015, when the campaign against the Islamic State was already in full swing, I listened to United Nations ambassador Susan Rice tell a room full of active-duty troops, including several severely injured soldiers, some missing legs or ears blown off in bomb blasts, that "one of our proudest accomplishments as an administration was ending the wars in Iraq and Afghanistan." Someone in the audience snorted in laughter. (It was clearly an administration talking point—two months later, the president claimed, "We've ended two wars.")

Afterward, I chatted with a furious, wheelchair-bound soldier with (partial) functionality in only one limb. He thought Rice had lied to our faces. But neither of us should have been surprised. Lying casually to the public about war is a privilege Americans have granted the executive branch.

Right now, it seems the president can do almost anything under the dangerously broad powers afforded him by the 2002 Authorization for the Use of Military Force. Under Obama, that meant airstrikes in support of Iranian-backed militias in Iraq, support for a war against Iranian-backed forces in Yemen, and whatever the hell our policy was in Syria, all at the same time, mostly against groups that didn't exist in 2002, while pretending we weren't at war anywhere. Under Trump, it means killing Iran's most important general on Iraqi soil. Who knows what it will mean for whoever holds office in 2021?

In 2014, when Congress was considering a new authorization for the fight against the Islamic State, advocacy groups insisted on a sunset clause, geographic limits, and reporting requirements to provide transparency about the mission, its progress, and its costs. But Congress did nothing, and so we have come to the present day—when, in a classified briefing Wednesday on Suleimani's death that even two Republican senators described as "un-American" and "an insult to the Constitution," the administration suggested that the president had no need for congressional approval of military action against Iran. (Late Thursday, the House passed new limits on Trump's war powers against Iran, but a similar measure is unlikely to pass in the Senate, and it's not clear how effective it would be if it did.)

With such anemic congressional oversight, is it any wonder our wars have been handled so poorly, that overseas conflicts grow out of control, and that the public notices only when disaster looms? A nation unwilling to hold itself accountable perhaps deserves incoherent policy. But the Iraqi people, who will bear the brunt of the coming violence, do not.

WAR, LOSS, AND
UNTHINKABLE YOUTH

MAY 30, 2016

A t Arlington National Cemetery, it was the birthdays that got to me. This was a couple of years ago, and my brother and I were visiting Section 60, where they put our generation of veterans.

I walked to the row of the newest graves and there, inscribed, I read: 1990. 1991. 1992. I stopped, startled by the unexpected dates. I don't know why, but it never really hit home for me until that moment that, of course, this war would eventually start eating the children of the '90s.

I was born in 1983, the year Michael Jackson released the music video for "Thriller." I'd gone to Iraq, come back, and left the Marine Corps before some of these kids had even been old enough to sign up. Kids born in the year of Madonna's "Vogue," James Cameron's *Terminator 2: Judgment Day*, Kriss Kross's "Jump."

This weekend I should be thinking about the Marines I know who died, all of them born in my decade. And I do. I think about them all the time. But Memorial Day always seemed to me to be a holiday best suited for healing wounds from past wars. Quiet reflection in a time of peace.

Who knows when that will happen? President Obama will likely end his time in office as the first U.S. president to spend the entirety of his two terms at war.

And since the conflicts overseas show little sign of dying down, this is the new normal. The kids joining the Marine Corps now, some of them as young as seventeen, have grown up in an America that, for as long as they've been aware of a world outside our borders, has been at war.

We try to ignore this unpleasant fact. We declared an end to combat mission in Iraq in 2010. The combat mission in Afghanistan supposedly ended in 2014. Still, we kept thousands of troops in both countries.

Their mission, we were told, "will not involve American combat troops fighting on foreign soil." They would conduct "supervise, train and assist" missions. They wouldn't constitute "boots on the ground."

So when they die, our government does what former defense secretary Robert Gates calls "semantic backflips" to avoid saying that our troops are in combat. At a recent press conference where journalists repeatedly asked the Pentagon press secretary whether or not we were "in combat," he had the unenviable job of explaining that, well, they're "in harm's way" or "in combat situations," or "they have found themselves under fire."

Such evasions grate on me, especially around Memorial Day. This year's war dead—nine so far—didn't slip, trip, and find themselves in combat. We sent them there to fight a war on our behalf, whether we like to acknowledge that or not. They went, they fought, and they died.

So my sadness this weekend, the same sadness I felt walking through Arlington, is mixed with something else. I can't simply reflect on the dead of my war. I can't simply memorialize.

Thinking through the legacy of my war carries with it the uncomfortable knowledge that, years after I left the Corps, we're still there. General George C. Marshall's claim that "a democracy cannot fight a Seven Years' War" has long since been disproven. We can, and we do—so long as it's fought by a fraction of the population and, for the most part, kept out of sight.

What remains to be seen is what a war that lasts so long does to a democracy, especially when so much of that war is conducted in the shadows. I already know some of what it does to those who serve.

Soon the first children of the 2000s will be able to sign up, the babies of the new millennium, of Destiny's Child's "Say My Name" and, appropriately enough, Ridley Scott's *Gladiator*. Give another year, and we may very well be seeing kids join up who've spent their whole lives in a country at war, whether we call it that or not.

Perhaps I'm wrong to focus on the dates. I suppose the year doesn't matter so much. When I think of the dead I knew, I always remember the words of a Vietnam veteran telling me about his best friend in the world, a sweet kid, a child of the 1950s, of the year of Miles Davis's "Birth of the Cool" and Hank Williams's "Long Gone Lonesome Blues."

He spoke very simply of his friend, what he was like and why he was the sort of guy you could count on, even if he might not have been the best soldier in the world. And then he looked up and told me, "He was nineteen, and he always will be."

II | CITIZENS

CITIZEN-SOLDIER: MORAL RISK AND THE MODERN MILITARY

MAY 24, 2016

T he rumor was he'd killed an Iraqi soldier with his bare hands. Or maybe bashed his head in with a radio. Something to that effect. Either way, during inspections at Officer Candidates School, the Marine Corps version of boot camp for officers, he was the sergeant instructor who asked the hardest, the craziest questions. No softballs. No, "Who's the Old Man of the Marine Corps?" or "What's your first general order?" The first time he paced down the squad bay, all of us at attention in front of our racks, he grilled the would-be infantry guys with, "Would it bother you, ordering men into an assault where you know some will die?" and the would-be pilots with, "Do you think you could drop a bomb on an enemy target, knowing you might also kill women and kids?"

When he got to me, down at the end, he unloaded one of his more involved hypotheticals. "All right, candidate. Say you think there's an insurgent in a house and you call in air support, but then when you

walk through the rubble there's no insurgents, just this dead Iraqi civilian with his brains spilling out of his head, his legs still twitching
and a little Iraqi kid at his side asking you why his father won't get up.
So. What are you going to tell that Iraqi kid?"

Amid all the playacting of OCS—screaming "Kill!" with every
movement during training exercises, singing cadences about how
tough we are, about how much we relish violence—this felt like a
valuable corrective. In his own way, that sergeant instructor was trying to clue us in to something few people give enough thought to
when they sign up: joining the Marine Corps isn't just about exposing
yourself to the trials and risks of combat—it's also about exposing
yourself to moral risk.

I never had to explain to an Iraqi child that I'd killed his father. As
a public affairs officer, working with the media and running an office
of Marine journalists, I was never even in combat. And my service in
Iraq was during a time when things seemed to be getting better. But
that period was just one small part of the disastrous war I chose to
have a stake in. "We all volunteered," a friend of mine and a five-tour
Marine veteran, Elliot Ackerman, said to me once. "I chose it and I
kept choosing it. There's a sort of sadness associated with that."

As a former Marine, I've watched the unraveling of Iraq with a
sense of grief, rage, and guilt. As an American citizen, I've felt the
same, though when I try to trace the precise lines of responsibility of
a civilian versus a veteran, I get all tangled up. The military ethicist
Martin Cook claims there is an "implicit moral contract between the
nation and its soldiers," which seems straightforward, but as the mission of the military has morphed and changed, it's hard to see what
that contract consists of. A decade after I joined the Marines, I'm left
wondering what obligations I incurred as a result of that choice, and
what obligations I share with the rest of my country to our wars and

to the men and women who fight them. What, precisely, was the bargain that I struck when I raised my hand and swore to defend my country against all enemies, foreign and domestic?

GRAND CAUSES

It was somewhat surprising (to me, anyway, and certainly to my parents) that I wound up in the Marines. I wasn't from a military family. My father had served in the Peace Corps, my mother was working in international medical development. If you'd asked me what I wanted to do postcollege, I would have told you I wanted to become a career diplomat, like my maternal grandfather. I had no interest in going to war.

Operation Desert Storm was the first major world event to make an impression on me—though to my seven-year-old self the news coverage showing grainy videos of smart bombs unerringly finding their targets made those hits seem less a victory of soldiers than a triumph of technology. The murky, muddy conflicts in Mogadishu and the Balkans registered only vaguely. War, to my mind, meant World War II, or Vietnam. The first I thought of as an epic success, the second as a horrific failure, but both were conflicts capable of capturing the attention of our whole society. Not something struggling for airtime against a presidential sex scandal.

So I didn't get my ideas about war from the news, or from the wars actually being fought during my teenage years. I got my ideas from books.

Reading novels or story collections like Joseph Heller's *Catch-22*, or Tim O'Brien's *The Things They Carried*, I learned to see war as pointless suffering, absurdity, a spectacle of man's inhumanity to man. Yet narrative nonfiction told me something different, particularly the narrative nonfiction about World War II, a genre really getting off the ground in the late 1990s and early aughts. Perhaps this was a belated result of the Gulf War, during which the military seemed to have shaken off its post-Vietnam malaise and shown that, yes, goddamn it, we can win something, and win it good. Books like Stephen Ambrose's *Band of Brothers* and Tom Brokaw's *The Greatest Generation* went hand in hand with movies like *Saving Private Ryan* to present a vision of remarkable heroism in a world that desperately needed it.

In short, my novels and my histories were sending very mixed signals. War was either pointless hell, or it was the shining example of American exceptionalism. In middle school, I'd read Ambrose's *Citizen Soldiers*, about the European Theater in World War II. More than anything else, it was the title that stayed with me, the notion of service in a grand cause as the extension of citizenship. I never bothered to consider that the mix of draftees and volunteers who served in World War II wasn't so different from the mix of draftees and volunteers who served in Vietnam, or that the atrocities committed in that war were no less horrific than those committed in Vietnam, though no one was likely to write a bestselling book about Vietnam entitled *Citizen Soldiers*. The title appealed to me. Deeply. But I didn't see any grand causes in the 1990s, just a series of messy, limited engagements. Of course, in the history of American warfare, from the Indian Wars to the Philippines to the Banana Wars, it was the grand causes that were the anomalies, not the brushfire wars at the edge of empire.

Then 9/11 happened. We all have our stories of where we were that day. Mine is that I was in the woods, hiking the Appalachian Trail. As my little group of hikers scrambled over the rough paths, we kept running into people telling stories of planes hitting the World Trade Center. It sounded preposterous, the sort of rumor that could easily spread in an isolated place, in the days before everybody had a smartphone. But we kept hearing the story, in ever more detail, until it became clear—particularly for those of us from New York—that we had to leave the woods.

I can't say that I joined the military because of 9/11. Not exactly. By the time I got around to it the main U.S. military effort had shifted to Iraq, a war I'd supported, though one I never associated with al-Qaeda or Osama bin Laden. But without 9/11, we might not have been at war there, and if we hadn't been at war, I wouldn't have joined.

It was a strange time to make the decision, or at least it seemed strange to many of my classmates and professors. I raised my hand and swore my oath of office on May 11, 2005. It was a year and a half after Saddam Hussein's capture. The weapons of mass destruction had not been found. The insurgency was growing. It wasn't just the wisdom of the invasion that was in doubt, but also the competence of the policy makers. Then–secretary of defense Donald Rumsfeld had been proven wrong about almost every major postinvasion decision, from troop levels to postwar reconstruction funds. Anybody paying close attention could tell that Iraq was spiraling into chaos, and the once jubilant public mood about our involvement in the war, with over 70 percent of Americans in 2003 nodding along in approval, was souring. But the potential for failure, and the horrific cost in terms of human lives that failure would entail, only underscored for me why I should do my part. This was my grand cause, my test of citizenship.

CITIZEN-SOLDIERS VERSUS "BASE HIRELINGS"

The highly professional all-volunteer force I joined, though, wouldn't have fit with the Founding Fathers' conception of citizen-soldiers.

They distrusted standing armies: Alexander Hamilton thought Congress should vote every two years "upon the propriety of keeping a military force on foot"; James Madison claimed "armies kept up under the pretext of defending, have enslaved the people"; and Thomas Jefferson suggested the Greeks and Romans were wise "to put into the hands of their rulers no such engine of oppression as a standing army."

They wanted to rely on "the people," not on professionals. According to the historian James Thomas Flexner, at the outset of the Revolutionary War George Washington had grounded his military thinking on the notion that "his virtuous citizen-soldiers would prove in combat superior, or at least equal, to the hireling invaders." This was an understandably attractive belief for a group of rebellious colonists with little military experience. The historian David McCullough tells us that the average American Continental soldier viewed the British troops as "hardened, battle-scarred veterans, the sweepings of the London and Liverpool slums, debtors, drunks, common criminals and the like, who had been bullied and beaten into mindless obedience."

Even lower in their eyes were the Hessian troops the British had hired to fight the colonists, which were commanded by Lieutenant-General Leopold Philip von Heister. A veteran of many campaigns, von Heister had crankily sailed over from England, touched shore, "called for hock and swallowed large potations to the health of his friends," and then, apparently, set out trying to kill Americans.

There's a long tradition of distrust of mercenaries, from Aristotle claiming they "turn cowards . . . when the danger puts too great a strain on them," to Machiavelli arguing they're "useless and dangerous . . . disunited, ambitious and without discipline, unfaithful, valiant before friends, cowardly before enemies," and the colonists would likely have agreed with such assessments. Mercenaries were at the bottom of the hierarchy of military excellence, citizen-soldiers at the top. We can see this view reflected in George Washington's message to his soldiers before the first major engagement of the Revolutionary War, the Battle of Long Island:

> Remember, officers and Soldiers, that you are Freemen. . . .
> Remember how your Courage and Spirit have been despised, and traduced by your cruel invaders, though they have found by dear experience at Boston, Charlestown and other places, what a few brave men contending in their own land, and in best of causes can do, against base hirelings and mercenaries.

This was in August 1776, and Washington's nineteen thousand men were about to see whether their civic virtues would triumph over British military skill. The American line stretched out across central Brooklyn, with British troops advancing from the south and the east. Though there was skirmishing during the day on August 26, the real fighting began the next morning, when a column of Hessians marched up Battle Pass, in modern-day Prospect Park.

What followed was a disaster. In the unkind phrasing of historian W. J. Wood, "Washington and his commanders . . . performed like ungifted amateurs," and that's exactly how the Hessian mercenaries viewed them. "The rebels had a very advantageous position in the wood," wrote one Hessian soldier, "but when we attacked them courageously in their hiding-places, they ran, as all mobs do." Colonel Heinrich von Heeringen, the commander of a Hessian regiment, wrote, "The riflemen were mostly spitted to the trees with bayonets. These frightful people deserve pity rather than fear." And looking over those he'd captured, von Heeringen sneered, "Among the prisoners are many so-called colonels, lieutenant-colonels, majors, and other officers, who, however, are nothing but mechanics, tailors, shoe-makers, wig-makers, barbers, etc. Some of them were soundly beaten by our people, who would by no means let such persons pass for officers."

It was a rough education for Washington. At the close of the war he would submit to Congress his "Sentiments on a Peace Establishment," which noted that "Altho' a *large* standing Army in time of Peace hath ever been considered dangerous to the liberties of a Country, yet a few Troops, under certain circumstances, are not only safe, but indispensably necessary." Congress, however, rejected the idea of even a modest standing army for the nation, its only concession being to keep one standing regiment and a battery of artillery. The rest of the new nation's defense would rely mostly on state militias. Hence the Second Amendment. This idealistic vision of militias as a bulwark of democracy would soon face a harsh reality check.

In this case, it was not the British but the Western Confederacy of American Indians who'd give the Americans their comeuppance. Mixed units of American regulars and militiamen had been fighting these tribes throughout the early 1790s. The first campaign, led by General Josiah Harmar, was meant "to chastise the Indian Nations who have of late been so troublesome." Today, the campaign is known as Harmar's Defeat, which tells you all you really need to know about whether or not that happened. The individual battles within that campaign don't have much better titles. There's Hardin's Defeat, Hartshorn's Defeat, the Battle of Pumpkin Fields. This last doesn't sound so bad, until you learn that it supposedly got its name not because it was fought in a pumpkin field, but because the steam from the scalped skulls of militiamen reminded the victorious American Indians of squash steaming in the autumn air.

Harmar was succeeded by General Arthur St. Clair, who, though rather old, rather fat, and afflicted with gout, set out with "sanguine expectations that a severe blow might be given to the savages yet." His poorly trained, undisciplined men engaged an equal-sized force at the Battle of the Wabash in November 1791, also known by the considerably more evocative title, the Battle of a Thousand Slain. What followed was the worst military disaster of U.S. history. Of St. Clair's 920 troops, 632 were killed and 264 wounded, a casualty rate of just over 97 percent. Congress, finally conceding that professionalism did count for something, bowed to the creation of a standing army beyond absolute bare bones.

Of course, the creation of the army hardly ended the complicated relationship Americans had with professional soldiers. When we come to the Civil War, the first war in which we instituted a national draft, none other than Ulysses S. Grant would call the professional soldiers who'd manned the army prior to the war "men who could not do as well in any other occupation." Naturally, he was not talking about his own men, fine citizen-soldiers who "risked life for a principle . . . often men of social standing, competence, or wealth and independence of character." It took a grand cause, then, like the Civil War, for military service to count as a civic virtue.

And not only was it a civic virtue—it could be what made you American in the first place. During World War I, Assistant Secretary of War Henry Breckinridge maintained that when immigrants and those born in this country rub "elbows in a common service to a common Fatherland . . . out comes the hyphen—up goes the Stars and Stripes. . . . Universal military service will be the elder brother of the public school in fusing this American race." During World War II, Franklin Delano Roosevelt thought military service would "Americanize" foreigners.

To this day, however, there continues to be a cynicism about the motives of those who volunteer for the military. I've been repeatedly told that people don't really enlist because they want to, but because they have to. I remember seeing the poet and playwright Maurice Decaul, frustrated with an insistent questioner who couldn't accept that an intelligent and sensitive soul might *want* to join the military, finally just blurt out, "I wanted to join the Marine Corps since I was eight years old." And all the veterans I know who are Ivy League graduates have had the unpleasant experience of people acting as though they'd made some sort of bizarre choice to spend time with the peons. At one event a Pulitzer Prize–winning journalist explained to me that, though he felt the Iraq War was evil, he didn't feel the soldiers should be blamed for their participation—they were only in service because they had no other options.

This is the "poverty draft"—the idea that with the elimination of the draft, we shifted the burden from the whole of society to only the most poor and disadvantaged, who join the military to get a step up in life and then become cannon fodder. The demographics of the military don't support the image—it's actually the middle class that's best represented in the military, and the numbers of high-income and highly educated recruits rose to levels disproportionate to their percentage of the population after the War on Terror began. But this notion of a military filled with ne'er-do-wells who are in it only for the money is frustrating not just because it's insulting or false—it takes the decision to put one's life at risk for one's country and transforms it, as if by magic, into a self-interested act. Veterans have a benefit package . . . they're paid in full, right? If the war was a just one and they saved the world against fascism, or slavery, maybe more is owed. If not, well, you can pity them, but you can't take them seriously as moral agents.

MESSING UP YOUR NICE, CLEAN SOUL

The decision to accept my commission was the most important one I'd made in my twenty-one years of life, and I knew it. I also knew I'd likely end up in Iraq, that the next four years would be bound up with a politically and morally contentious conflict, and I was comfortable with that. But in 2005, it didn't seem to me that my decision about whether or not to join would make me any the more or less responsible for a war that had started in 2003. There's a bit in John Osborne's play *Look Back in Anger* where a character angrily tells his wife:

> It's no good trying to fool yourself about love. You can't fall into it like a soft job without dirtying up your hands. It takes muscle and guts. If you can't bear the thought of messing up your nice, clean soul you better give up the whole idea of life, and become a saint. Because you'll never make it as a human being.

As in love, so in politics. Choices have to be made, without the benefit of hindsight, and then you have to live with those choices. The chain of events begun with the invasion of Iraq would neither end nor alter through my own inaction. So when friends would argue with me about WMDs or the initial invasion it seemed radically beside the point. I didn't have a time machine; neither did they. Nor could I write off the entire war effort as evil and thereby evade any feeling of responsibility for all the policy decisions that came later.

Back in 2006, as I was preparing to go to Anbar Province, the "lost" province, the heart of the Sunni insurgency, it was tempting to think there was nothing we could do to improve the situation in Iraq, or even that doing nothing was somehow the best course of action. The following year, Senator Carl Levin would propose a rapid withdrawal in order to somehow magically force an Iraqi political settlement. "It is time for Congress to explain to the Iraqis that it is your country," he said in a speech before Congress, apparently under the impression that the Iraqis didn't know that. To me, this proposal for ending the occupation seemed little more than a smokescreen to allow us to leave Iraq behind without feeling too guilty about it.

Though the word *occupation* is often bandied about as though it represents something inherently evil, occupation is actually a situation legitimized—and circumscribed—by international law. Article 43 of the Hague Regulations of 1907 demands that an occupying force "shall take all the measures in [its] power to restore and ensure, as far as possible, public order and safety." Further obligations are spelled out in the Fourth Geneva Convention of 1949. These apply regardless of whether the war waged against the occupied country was just or unjust. We waged a just war against Germany and Japan during World War II and yet afterward still had an obligation to provide order for those countries' citizens, many of whom were starving, homeless refugees. For me, it didn't follow that *because* a war was unjust we were thereby relieved of our obligations as a country and could happily leave Iraqis to their sorry fate, secure in the knowledge that our hands were clean as long as we hadn't voted for George W. Bush in 2000. We obviously hadn't lived up to our obligations to prevent chaos in the aftermath of our invasion of Iraq.

Of course, none of that means that the deployment I was about to go on would, in fact, be part of an adequate or just national response to the tragedy unfolding there.

WE CAN TELL THEM THE TRUTH WHEN WE GET HOME

In the first month of my deployment, a suicide truck bomber detonated among a group of families going to mosque. United States' forces brought the injured into our base hospital, where the line of Marines waiting to give blood was so long that it extended out the door and wrapped around the building. Inside there were so many injured that the doctors ran out of trauma tables and had to do surgery on the floor. In one room, I saw them slowly stitching a man's intestines back together. In another, a surgeon new to the theater hesitated before a man's bloody, shrapnel-filled body. Time being of the essence, a doctor who'd been there several months already pushed him away, stuck a finger into the man's side, plunged it knuckle deep, and pulled out a jagged piece of metal from his abdomen.

Not much later a similar attack hit Ramadi. One of my Marines, a videographer, asked if he could interview one of our doctors after the attack. The only quiet place was where they were keeping the bodies of the dead, so the two sat in a corner, surrounded by civilian bodies, the men, women, and children the doctors hadn't been able to save. There, in the silence, the exhausted doctor wept.

The units moving out of theater around this time—doctors, infantryman, engineers, and logisticians—had seen a lot of violence, but not much progress. I remember listening in on an outgoing group of soldiers talking about what they should tell their families back home about the war. They couldn't tell them the truth, they agreed. Instead, they'd tell them proud, uplifting things. "We can tell them the truth when we get home," one said. It was quiet a moment, and another asked, "Will we even tell the truth then?"

That was early 2007. By 2008, violence had fallen, markets were opening, and police forces were swelling. The slowdown in death threw opponents of the U.S. troop surge for a loop. MoveOn.org famously suggested General David Petraeus was "cooking the books." More thoughtful critics came up with other responses: the gains were temporary, dependent on a political solution, or on untrustworthy allies, or on arming one side in a civil war. Or, less plausibly, given the actual patterns of violence in Iraq, maybe sectarian cleansing had sorted the country into Sunni and Shia enclaves and so the violence had declined only because there was no one left to kill. Even today, whether the surge "worked" is the subject of a fairly intense debate both within the military and outside of it. It's clear the Anbar Awakening—the Sunni revolt against al-Qaeda in Iraq—could not have reshaped the country in the way it did without significant U.S. support. But those who argue that the surge didn't solve Iraq's underlying issues are, of course, completely correct, and whether the Bush administration was right to pursue the surge in 2007 remains up for debate. Either way, it wasn't enough.

I didn't know that in 2008. I went home feeling great about my deployment. Iraq was getting better, and I'd been part of the force (even if a rear-echelon part) that had risked life and limb for that goal. And the good news kept coming. A year and a half after I got back, *The New York Times* had a story about a giant beach party thrown on the banks of Lake Habbaniyah, near where I'd spent much of my time overseas. Photos showed hundreds of young Iraqis having fun. A DJ yelled into a microphone: "Shoutout to everyone from Baghdad. Everyone from Adhamiyah and Sadr City." I spoke with another Marine who'd spent time in that area—the author Michael Pitre. He told me, "I remember reading that article and thinking, My God, did we win?"

I hoped so. Either way, I didn't feel I had anything to account for. I was under the impression that history had justified me. And though I'm a Catholic, it never even occurred to me to do something once common for soldiers after war—seek atonement.

In the medieval period, Christian theology carved out a space for war—what we now call "just war theory." Nevertheless, killing was still considered a sin, even in a just war, even when lawful, even when the Church itself had directed you to do it. One of the more remarkable consequences of this belief is the Penitential Ordinance imposed on Norman knights who fought with William the Conqueror on Senlac Hill at the Battle of Hastings in 1066. "Anyone who knows that he killed a man in the great battle must do penance for one year for each man that he killed," it proclaims, before moving forward and really getting into the weeds. If you wounded a man and aren't sure he died, forty days' penance. If you fought only for gain, it's the same penance as if you'd committed a regular homicide. For archers, "who killed some and wounded others, but are necessarily ignorant as to how many," three Lents' worth of penance.

To modern, rational ears, there seems something bizarre, if not cruel, about demanding something of men and then demanding penance for that same thing. And yet it is perhaps healthier both for the society that sends men to war and for the warriors themselves. Vietnam veteran Karl Marlantes, looking back on his time overseas, described himself "struggling with a situation approaching the sacred in its terror and contact with the infinite." Though he didn't know it then, what he desperately wanted was a spiritual guide. "We cannot expect normal eighteen-year-olds to kill someone and contain it in a healthy way. They must be helped to sort out what will be healthy grief about taking a life because it is part of the sorrow of war."

This route might offer not only redemption, but also genuine growth as a human being. The philosopher and World War II veteran

J. Glenn Gray wrote that for a soldier, "guilt can teach him, as few things else are able to, how utterly a man can be alienated from the very sources of his being. But the recognition may point the way to a reunion and a reconciliation with the varied forms of the created. . . . Atonement will become for him not an act of faith or a deed, but a life, a life devoted to strengthening the bonds between men and between man and nature."

But this is a way of thinking distinctly at odds with stories of uncomplicated military glory. "The notion of war as sin simply doesn't play in Peoria—or anywhere else in the United States—because a fondness for war is an essential component of the macho American God," wrote Vietnam War chaplain William Mahedy. "Yet the awareness of evil—in religious terms of consciousness of sin—is the underlying motif of the Vietnam War stories." And of course, it's not just Vietnam. This is a recurrent theme in writing from both the wars we celebrate and the wars we condemn. During an interview, I once cautiously asked a ninety-one-year-old veteran of World War II what he thought of the idea of the Greatest Generation. "It's bullshit!" he shouted, cutting me off. "Bullshit . . . War ruined my life." He later calmed and revised his self-assessment: "I'm eighty percent sweet and twenty percent bitter." And the twenty percent of bitterness that he still held with him, over seven decades later, came from his experiences in what we like to think of as "the Good War."

In terms of the contract young Marines and soldiers sign when joining the service, this moral dimension can be added to the physical and emotional risks they assume, risks present regardless of how we later come to feel about the particular war we send them off to. "Men wash their hands, in blood, as best they can," wrote the poet Randall Jarrell. Coming back from Iraq, with none of the memories of visceral horror we associate with the authentic experience of war, I assumed my hands were clean. As a staff officer, I had the privilege of seeing the war mostly as a spectator, the same privilege enjoyed by the rest of the American public—that is, if they bothered to look.

A SAVING IDEA?

Not long after ISIS had made headlines by seizing Fallujah and Ramadi, I went to the screening of a documentary about Afghanistan. During the Q&A with the director afterward, one of the many veterans there stood up. He was a big, tough-looking guy, must have been the perfect image of a Marine in dress blues. He said, "I'm a veteran of Iraq. That used to be something I was incredibly proud of. If you'd asked me, just a few years ago, to make a résumé of my life—not a résumé for a job, but a résumé of who I was, what I was—all the biggest bullet points would have been: Marine sergeant; combat veteran; led Marines in Iraq. But now, I'm looking at what's happening in Iraq, and I'm starting to wonder what I was a part of, and whether I can be proud of it. Was I part of an evil thing? Because if I was, then I don't know who I am anymore. I don't know what my identity is."

It was a sharper-edged response to the overseas tragedy than I'd previously heard. Though I'd seen many veterans wondering, "What was this all for?" they often resolved the question by narrowing their focus. One veteran who served in the Second Battle of Fallujah argued that he didn't think about "Bush or Obama, or about Iraq or Afghanistan," but about the men he'd served with and "what we'd done for each other." Elizabeth Samet, an instructor at West Point, argues that our recent wars' "absence of a clear and consistent political vision . . . forced many of the platoon leaders and company commanders I know to understand the dramas in which they found themselves as local and individual rather than national or communal. The ends they furnish for themselves—coming home without losing any soldiers or, if someone has to die, doing so heroically in battle—offer exclusively personal and particular consolations that make the mission itself effectively beside the point."

In its own way, American pop culture, with its increasing obsession with Special Forces conducting commando-style raids, seems to have come to a similar conclusion. *Zero Dark Thirty*, *13 Hours*, and *American Sniper* offer a vision of war in which highly trained operatives kill undoubtedly evil people—bomb makers and torturers and sadists and thugs of all stripes—without forcing too much consideration about the overall outcome. In a raid, the moral stakes seem clear. Let's think only about killing "the Butcher," or the evil enemy sniper, or Osama bin Laden, not about ending the chaos swirling around them. And though these movies have the veneer of nonfiction, their impact isn't so different from the previous generation's Rambo franchise, which Vietnam veteran and author Gustav Hasford argued "satisfies our pathetic need to win the war and gives us another coat of whitewash as bumbling do-gooders, innocent American white-bread boy[s], pulled down into corruption by wicked Orientals. We *should* have won, and we *could* have won, *Rambo* argues, if only the dumb grunts could have been saved by grotesquely muscled civilians who somehow skated the shooting war."

This kind of thinking has become operative not just in the movies but in real life. At his State of the Union Address, President Obama proclaimed earlier this year, "If you doubt America's commitment—or mine—to see that justice is done, just ask Osama bin Laden. Ask the leader of al-Qaeda in Yemen, who was taken out last year, or the perpetrator of the Benghazi attacks." He received applause, and it's not hard to understand why. Since these kinds of missions don't put troops in the position of holding territory, when we kill or capture a target we can mark that off as a success regardless of whether or not we're making a positive impact on the region we're striking. Never mind what's actually happening on the ground in Libya and Yemen right now. If you narrow your scope sufficiently, there's no end to what you don't have to deal with.

It's true that, in the middle of a deployment, the specifics of any individual unit's experience and the bonds those Marines share might overshadow their sense of the broader mission. But people join the military to be a part of something greater than themselves, and ultimately it's deeply important for service members to be able to feel their sacrifices had a purpose.

Pat C. Hoy II, a New York University professor who served in Vietnam, once described the aftermath of a battle in Vietnam waged by soldiers he'd trained. It had gratified him to see those soldiers recover "through the saving rituals they performed together—burying the dead, policing the battlefield, stacking ammunition, burning leftover powder bags, hauling trash, shaving, drinking coffee, washing, talking as they restored order and looked out for one another's welfare." These are the kind of small moments of communal satisfaction that I saw veteran after veteran invoke as they tried to come to terms with the extent of our failure in Iraq. For Hoy, such satisfactions are real, but insufficient.

Those men had done the soldiers' dirty job in a war that will probably never end—for them or for this nation. The Vietnam War will not be transfigured by a purifying idea. The men and women who fought there will forever be haunted by the fact of carnage itself. The ones who actually looked straight into the eyes of death will scream out in the middle of the night and awake shaking in cold sweat for the rest of their lives—and there will be no idea, nothing save the memory of teamwork, to redeem them. That will not be enough. That loneliness is what they get in return for their gift of service to a nation that sent them out to die and abandoned them to their own saving ideas when they came home.

What is the saving idea of Iraq? In some ways, joining the military is an act of faith in one's country—an act of faith that the country will use your life well. What your piece of a war will be, after all, is mostly a matter of chance. I have friends who joined prior to 9/11, when machine-gun instructors still taught recruits to depress the trigger as long as it takes to say, "Die, commie, die!" I have friends who joined after 9/11, expecting to fight al-Qaeda, only to invade Iraq. One friend protested the Iraq War, then signed up *because* he felt the war was unjust and so we owed the Iraqis a humane, responsible occupation. The army sent him to Afghanistan twice. Another soldier I know, a reservist, had a unit slotted for one of two deployments—either to help with the Ebola crisis, a mission few would object to, or to man Guantánamo Bay. Depending on where they were sent, they knew they'd face radically different reactions when they came home. Of course, the praise or censure your average American civilian might dole out to those soldiers would in reality just be the doling out of the praise or censure they themselves deserve for being part of a nation that does such things.

The difference, though, is that it's impossible for the veteran to pretend he has clean hands. No number of film dramatizations of commandos killing bad guys can move us past the simple reality that Iraq is destroyed, there is untold suffering overseas, and we as a country have even abandoned most of the translators who risked their lives for us.

Yet this fact seems not to have penetrated either the civilians we come home to or the government that sent us: "How many American presidents or members of Congress have suffered from PTSD or taken their own lives rather than live any longer with the burden of having declared a war?" asked humanities professor Robert Emmet Meagher. None, of course.

TOTAL MOBILIZATION

When my cell phone buzzed in a Brooklyn bar and the voice at the other end told me a Marine I'd served with had been shot in Afghanistan, I looked around, searching for someone to talk to. The band setting up, the tattooed bartenders, any of them could have plausibly been a sympathetic ear. I've generally found civilians quite interested once you take the effort. And yet . . . I couldn't. It would, I suspected, be treated as a personal tragedy, as though I were delivering the news that a family member had been diagnosed with cancer. Not as something that implicated them.

There's a joke among veterans, "Well, we were winning Iraq when *I* was there," and the reason it's a joke is because to be in the military is to be acutely conscious of how much each person relies on the larger organization. In boot camp, to be called "an individual" is a slur. A Marine on his or her own is not a militarily significant unit. At the Basic School, the orders we were taught to write always included a lost Marine plan, which means every order given carries with it the implicit message: you are nothing without the group. The Bowe Bergdahl case is a prime example of what happens when one soldier takes it upon himself to find the war he felt he was owed—a chance to be like the movie character Jason Bourne, as Bergdahl explained on tapes played by the podcast *Serial*. The intense anger directed at Bergdahl from rank-and-file soldiers, an anger sometimes hard for a civilian public raised on notions of American individualism to comprehend, is the anger of a collective whose members depend on each other for their very lives directed toward one who, through sheer self-righteous idiocy, violated the intimate bonds of camaraderie. By abandoning his post in Afghanistan, Bergdahl made his fellow soldiers' brutally hard, dangerous, and possibly futile mission even harder and more dangerous and more futile, thereby breaking the cardinal rule of military life: Don't be a buddy fucker. You are not the hero of this movie.

But a soldier doesn't just rely on his squadmates, or on the leadership of his platoon and company. There's close air support, communications, and logistics. Reliable weapons, ammunition, and supplies. The entire apparatus of war—all of it ultimately resting on American industry and on the tax dollars that each of us pays. "The image of war as armed combat merges into the more extended image of a gigantic labor process," wrote Ernst Jünger, a German writer and veteran of World War I. After the Second World War, Kurt Vonnegut would come to a similar conclusion, reflecting not only on the planes and crews, the bullets and bombs and shell fragments, but also where those came from: the factories "operating night and day," the transportation lines for the raw materials, and the miners working to extract them. Think too hard about the frontline soldier, you end up thinking about all that was needed to put him there.

Today, we're still mobilized for war, though in a manner perfectly designed to ensure we don't think about it too much. Since we have an all-volunteer force, participation in war is a matter of choice, not a requirement of citizenship, and those in the military represent only a tiny fraction of the country—what historian Andrew Bacevich calls "the 1 percent army." So the average civilian's chance of knowing any member of the service is correspondingly small.

Moreover, we're expanding those aspects of warfighting that fly under the radar. Our drone program continues to grow, as does the Special Operations Forces community, which has expanded from 45,600 Special Forces personnel in 2001 to 70,000 today, with further increases planned. The average American is even less likely to know a drone pilot or a member of a Special Ops unit—or to know much about what they actually do, either, since you can't embed a reporter with a drone or with SEAL Team Six. Our Special Operations Command has become, in the words of former lieutenant colonel John Nagl, "an almost industrial-scale counterterrorism killing machine."

Though it's true that citizens do vote for the leaders who run this machine, we've absolved ourselves from demanding a serious debate about it in Congress. We're still operating under a decade-old Authorization for Use of Military Force issued in the wake of 9/11, before some of the groups we're currently fighting even existed, and it's unlikely, despite attempts from Senators Tim Kaine and Jeff Flake, that Congress will issue a new one any time soon. We wage war "with or without congressional action," in the words of President Obama at his final State of the Union Address, which means that the American public remains insulated from considering the consequences. Even if they voted for the president ordering these strikes, there's seemingly little reason for citizens to feel personally culpable when they go wrong.

It's that sense of a personal stake in war that the veteran experiences viscerally, and which is so hard for the civilian to feel. The philosopher Nancy Sherman has explained postwar resentment as resulting from a broken contract between society and the veterans who serve. "They may feel guilt toward themselves and resentment at commanders for betrayals," she writes, "but also, more than we are willing to acknowledge, they feel resentment toward us for our indifference toward their wars and afterwars, and for not even having to bear the burden of a war tax for over a decade of war. Reactive emotions, like resentment or trust, presume some kind of community—or at least are invocations to reinvoke one or convoke one anew."

The debt owed them, then, is not simply one of material benefits. There's a remarkable piece in *Harper's Magazine* titled "It's Not That I'm Lazy," published in 1946 and signed by an anonymous veteran, that argues, "There's a kind of emptiness inside me that tells me that I've still got something coming. It's not a pension that I'm looking for. What I paid out wasn't money; it was part of myself. I want to be paid back in kind, in something human."

That sounds right to me: "something human," though I'm not sure what form it would take. When I first came back from Iraq, I thought it meant a public reckoning with the war, with its costs not just for Americans but for Iraqis as well. As time goes by, and particularly as I watch a U.S. presidential debate in which candidates have offered up carpet-bombing, torture, and other kinds of war crimes as the answer to complex problems that the military has long since learned will only worsen if we attempt such simplistic and immoral solutions, I've given up on hoping that will happen anytime soon. If the persistence of U.S. military bases named after Confederate generals is any indication, it might not happen in my lifetime. The Holocaust survivor Jean Améry, considering Germany's postwar rehabilitation, would conclude, "Society . . . thinks only about its continued existence." Decades later, Ta-Nehisi Coates, considering the difficulty, if not impossibility, of finding solutions for various historic tragedies, would write, "I think we all see our 'theories and visions' come to dust in the 'starving, bleeding, captive land' which is everywhere, which is politics."

BRINGING THE MISSION HOME

Despite this, I don't see nihilism from my fellow veterans. I see the opposite. I've met veterans who, horrified by the human cost of our wars overseas, have joined groups like the International Refugee Assistance Project or the International Rescue Committee. I've met veterans who've gone into public service—one of whom also remained in a reserve unit because, as he put it to me, "I want to know the decisions I make might affect me personally." I've met veterans who've lobbied Congress, worked to fight military sexual assault, established literary nonprofits, or worked to make public service—military or otherwise—an expectation within American society. A recent analysis of Census data shows that, compared with their peers, veterans volunteer more, give more to charity, vote more often, and are more likely to attend community meetings and join civic groups. This is the kind of civic engagement necessary for the functioning of a democracy.

In 2007, Rhodes Scholar and Navy SEAL Eric Greitens made a visit to the National Naval Medical Center in Bethesda, Maryland. The men and women he found there, including amputees and serious burn victims, generally were eager to return to their units, though that would in many cases be impossible. These vets had been repeatedly thanked for their service. They'd been assured they were heroes and that they had the support of a grateful nation. But, as recounted in Joe Klein's book *Charlie Mike*, Greitens found what energized them was something different. Four words: "We still need you."

Greitens, who is hoping to win the Republican nomination in the Missouri governor's race this year, went on to found The Mission Continues, an organization that awards community-service fellowships that "redeploy" post-9/11 veterans back to their communities to work on projects from education to housing and beyond. One study found that, though these veterans had high rates of traumatic brain injury (52 percent), PTSD (64 percent) and depression (28 percent), the opportunity to feel that they had made a contribution led to remarkably positive postfellowship experiences. Eighty-six percent reported that the fellowship was a positive, life-changing experience. Seventy-one percent went on to pursue further education, 86 percent transferred their military skills to civilian employment, and large majorities reported that the fellowships helped them become community leaders able to teach others the value of service.

"While most watch the suffering of the world on their TV, we ACT, rapidly and with great purpose," wrote Marine sniper Clay Hunt, a veteran of Iraq and Afghanistan who provided relief efforts with the veteran-led disaster response organization Team Rubicon in the wake of earthquakes in Chile and Haiti, raised money for wounded veterans, and helped lobby Congress for veterans' benefits. "Not counting the cost and without hope for reward. We simply refuse to watch our world suffer, when we have the skills and the means to alleviate some of that suffering, for as many people as we can reach. . . . Inaction is not an option."

STRENGTHENING THE BONDS BETWEEN MEN AND BETWEEN MAN AND NATURE

Clay Hunt took his own life in March 2011. His story may be a heroic tale of a Marine who served with distinction and came home determined to continue serving, but it is also the much darker story of a Marine who was never able to get the help he himself needed. Once out of the Corps, Hunt struggled with the Veterans Administration over his disability rating and his treatment. He appealed the low level of his benefits only to face one bureaucratic hurdle after another, including the VA losing his files, the process dragging out for eighteen months. As for his medical care, he got almost no counseling for his post-traumatic stress, but was instead prescribed a variety of drugs, none of which seemed to help. He felt he'd been used as a "guinea pig" for one failed treatment after another. After moving to Houston, he waited months for his first appointment with a psychiatrist, and then found the appointment so stressful he resolved never to return. Two weeks later he killed himself.

True integration back into society can be overwhelmingly difficult for veterans struggling with unbearable physical or mental injuries. Hence the bare minimum of the payment veterans are due: a reliable Veterans Administration, improved mental health care, and adequate help transitioning to the civilian sector. The Clay Hunt Suicide Prevention for American Veterans (SAV) Act that President Obama signed into law in 2015 is intended to address some of these needs.

But this is just a starting place. It does not fully repay the debt to a Marine suffering post-traumatic stress if we provide him access to competent mental health care, just as we don't fully repay the debt to a soldier who lost a limb by handing her a well-made prosthetic. And in the wake of a war that has left whole societies shattered, hundreds of thousands of lives lost and more displaced, the debt cannot be solely to an individual, or even to a class of individuals, like veterans. A therapeutic approach, however necessary, can only heal wounds. Our problems run deeper than that.

I began this essay contemplating the oath I swore as a Marine to support and defend the Constitution. At the time I took the oath it felt like a special and precious burden I was taking on—sworn to defend not simply the physical security of my homeland but to defend something broader, our founding document, and thus the set of ideals embedded within it. Years later, looking through the section in the U.S. Citizenship and Immigration Services' "Citizen's Almanac" on citizens' responsibilities, I was embarrassed to realize my obligations as a Marine were not so unique. The very first responsibility listed is to "support and defend the Constitution against all enemies, foreign and domestic." So I had already owed that to my country, by virtue of my birth and the privilege of being American.

The divide between the civilian and the service member, then, need not feel so wide. Perhaps the way forward is merely through living up to those ideals through action, and a greater commitment by the citizenry to the institutions of American civic life that so many veterans are working to rebuild. Teddy Roosevelt once claimed a healthy society would regard the man "who shirks his duty to the State in time of peace as being only one degree worse than the man who thus shirks it in time of war. A great many of our men . . . rather plume themselves upon being good citizens if they even vote; yet voting is the very least of their duties." That seems right to me. The exact nature of those additional duties will depend on the individual's principles. What is undeniable, though, is that there is always a way to serve, to help bend the power and potential of the United States toward the good.

No civilian can assume the moral burdens felt at a gut level by participants in war, but all can show an equal commitment to their country, an equal assumption of the obligations inherent in citizenship, and an equal bias for action. Ideals are one thing; the messy business of putting them into practice is another. That means giving up on any claim to moral purity. That means getting your hands dirty.

THE GOOD WAR

JULY 5, 2013

A few years ago I attended a party for World War II veterans, held at a friend's home on the anniversary of D-Day. It was a relatively sedate affair: a few surprisingly short men from the Greatest Generation sitting around trading stories about work and life—not much talk of war. Then one of the men, Tony, brought out a book of his photographs, black-and-white snaps he'd taken while he was with the 83rd Infantry.

The photographs were, by turns, fascinating and beautiful and horrible, as war photos tend to be. And then I encountered one that looked less like an image of battle than of a crime scene. Almost casually, Tony pointed to the photo, leaned over toward me, and started talking about it. None of the other veterans paid much attention, as if they'd heard the story already, and Tony was nonchalant, as though his story wouldn't be any particular revelation. It was a part of his war, the "Good War," and he'd been living with it for sixty-five years.

The image showed a beautiful woman in an elegant dress—"fine silks," Tony told me—lying in blood, her legs twisted under her. It could have been one of Weegee's portraits of murder victims from the 1930s Lower East Side, except she had an antitank rocket, almost as long as she was, lying beside her.

Tony had come upon her on May 8, 1945, the day of the German surrender. She had been disarmed before she could fire, and then raped. Tony pointed out one particularly grisly detail of the photo: "You see here. This is a knife. The handle of the knife is dark, you see. Then you see gray, and a little white, there. OK. This gray is red blood. That knife was stuck in her vagina. Now, if she was dead, that blood would not be there. Do you understand? The blood was running, which means she was still alive when someone stuck that thing in her and killed her. . . . And I cried. Tears came to my eyes. But one of the problems was her. She was ready to knock out an American tank . . .

"So kill her but . . . This hurt me. Because it showed me how little mankind is in 1945."

Tony explained he felt obliged to photograph the woman, to document what had happened. There was little hope there'd be any other acknowledgment of the crime or punishment for her rapists and murderers. Before he took the picture, though, he removed the knife from between her legs. He wanted to leave her some dignity while still recording the event. Almost immediately, he felt he'd done something wrong. Sanitized the scene. He held the knife in his hand, understood that putting it back was beyond his capacities, and lay it on the ground by her left shoulder. Then he took his photo.

This was not the kind of story I expected to hear that night. I've read enough military history to know such events are not uncommon during wartime, and the recently published *What Soldiers Do*, about the wave of rapes by GIs in France in 1944–45, attests that they were hardly uncommon even when GIs were among the Allied population, but I didn't expect anything like Tony's story to come out, to me, on a night like that. It felt horrific, shameful, and abhorrent. If someone else had told the story, not a veteran and witness but a civilian, I would have felt they were being crass, even dishonorable. I would have suspected them of narrow-minded political motives. Maybe, if I was feeling especially piqued, I would have argued that such events were rare, and that such an act, awful as it was, was nothing compared to the abuses of the Nazis or the Soviets.

But Tony had been there.

Thirty-eight years ago, literary critic and World War II veteran Paul Fussell argued that soldiers often refuse to tell their war stories because they "have discovered that no one is very interested in the bad news they have to report." Fifteen years ago, Steven Spielberg felt the need to justify his inclusion of a momentary depiction of American soldiers executing surrendering enemy troops in *Saving Private Ryan*, because even in a film that for the most part glorifies the war and the Americans who fought it, these token moments of atrocity were too much for some viewers. "I don't want to turn Americans away from the patriotism many of us feel," he said, "but in the process of the chaos of combat, these were some of the things men were driven to do."

After the fighting is done and even when it's still happening, apologies are often needed for the recounting of bare facts. Sometimes bare facts feel unpatriotic.

So why report those facts? Isn't it more important that these are the men who stormed the beaches at D-Day, lifted the flag at Iwo Jima, and liberated Auschwitz? As of this writing, five of the top ten bestselling history books on Amazon are about World War II. The publishers' descriptions of these books are telling. One is a story of "survival, resilience, and redemption." Another, about women who contributed to the Manhattan Project, describes "their pluck, their desire to contribute, and their enduring courage." Another is an "incredible true story of combat and chivalry," and another is a "chronicle of the war that unshackled a continent and preserved freedom in the West." I'm sure these are all excellent books—and also that it's no accident that the bestsellers are paeans to national greatness and the courage and honor of our soldiers.

It's no wonder then that Iraq vets like myself still feel under the shadow of World War II. Valor and resilience and triumphs of the human spirit abound in stories of Iraq (just look up Bradley Kasal or Jason Dunham or Ross McGinnis or Paul R. Smith), but their stories are off on the side somewhere, along with similar ones from the other American wars about which we aren't allowed to feel unabashed pride. Korea, I suppose, is the forgotten war, Vietnam the bad war, the Persian Gulf the blink-and-you-missed-it war, and Iraq, as our president famously put it, the stupid war.

At a panel discussion with other veteran authors discussing our recent anthology of veterans' fiction, *Fire and Forget*, one of the participants talked about the moral ambiguity of the Iraq War as contrasted with the clarity of World War II. I couldn't help but think of that story of the German woman. My war, during which the Marines I worked with desperately tried to restore order to a society in the grip of a savagely violent insurgency, is ambiguous. World War II, during which we interned our own Japanese American citizens, conducted systematic area bombing of civilians, regularly killed enemy prisoners of war and mutilated war dead, and perpetrated a shocking number of rapes in both the European and Pacific theaters, is unambiguous.

Without excusing any abuses committed in Iraq, such as the widespread use of torture in interrogations, it's fairly clear that modern

American soldiers have behaved with notable restraint and professionalism. Which makes sense. These wars are fought with an all-volunteer professional military under the often critical eye of both national and international press. The First Battle of Fallujah was called off in part because of the intensity of non-U.S. media coverage of civilian casualties from outlets like Al Jazeera. This is a far cry from the days when, as Paul Fussell put it, "No Marine was fully persuaded of his manly adequacy who didn't have a well-washed Japanese skull to caress and who didn't have a go at treating surrendering Japs as rifle targets."

I'm not antiwar. I served in a war, and I served proudly. But just or not, necessary or not, war is the industrial-scale slaughter of other humans. Which is perhaps why historical memory of war is so often at odds with the lived experience.

I don't believe in any Greatest Generation. I believe in great events. They sweep ordinary people up, expose them to extremes of human behavior and unimaginable tests of integrity and courage, and then deposit them back on the home front. Which is when we start telling ourselves stories about what it all meant.

DUTY AND PITY

MAY 23, 2014

A couple of years ago, I spoke at a storytelling competition about some Marines I'd known during our deployment in Iraq and my feelings on getting out of the Corps. After I left the stage, an older woman in the crowd came up to me and, without asking, started rubbing my back. Startled, I looked over at her. "It was very brave of you to tell that story," she said.

"Oh, thank you," I said, a little confused by what was happening. "I'm OK."

She smiled sympathetically but didn't stop. I wasn't sure what to do, so I turned to watch the next performer—and she remained behind me, rubbing me down as if I were a startled horse in a thunderstorm.

It was my first really jarring experience with an increasingly common reaction to my war stories: pity. I never thought anyone would pity me because of my time in the Marine Corps. I'd grown up in the era of the Persian Gulf War, when the U.S. military shook off its post-Vietnam malaise with a startlingly decisive victory and Americans eagerly consumed stories about the Greatest Generation and the Good War through books like *Citizen Soldiers* by Stephen Ambrose and movies like *Saving Private Ryan*. Joining the military was an admirable decision that earned you respect.

Early on in the Iraq War, after I accepted my commission in 2005, most people did at the very least seem impressed—*You ever fire those huge machine guns? Think you could kick those dudes' asses? Did you kill anyone?* I'd find myself in a bar back home on leave listening to some guy a few years out of college explaining apologetically that "I was totally gonna join the military, you know, but . . ." The usual stereotype projected onto me was that of a battle-hardened hero, which I'm not.

But as the Iraq War's approval levels sunk from 76 percent and ticker-tape parades to 40 percent and quiet forgetfulness, that flattering but inaccurate assumption has shifted to the notion that I'm damaged. Occasionally, someone will even inform me that I have post-traumatic stress disorder. They're never medical professionals, just strangers who've learned that I served.

One man told me that Iraq veterans "are all gonna snap in ten years" and so, since I'd been back for three years, I had seven left. Another, after I'd explained that I didn't suffer from PTSD and that my deployment as a staff officer in Iraq had been mild, said that I needed to have an honest conversation with myself. And since I'm a writer, I've been asked more times than I can count whether my writing is an act of therapy.

I'm never offended; these are genuinely concerned people trying to reach out. But I find it all strange, especially since the assumption never seems to be that I have the actual *symptoms* of PTSD—intrusive memories of some traumatic event, numbing behaviors, a state of persistent hyperarousal. Instead, it is more in line with the Iraq veteran Brian Van Reet's observation that "PTSD has graduated from a diagnosis into an idiom used by soldiers and civilians to talk about all kinds of suffering, loss, grief, guilt, rage, and unrewarded sacrifice." For a certain subset of the population, my service means that I—along with all other veterans—must be, in some ill-defined way, broken.

I suppose it is the lot of soldiers and Marines to be objectified according to the politics of the day and the mood of the American people about their war. I know a veteran of World War II who hates the idea of the Greatest Generation. "War ruined my life," he told me. "I couldn't date girls after the war. I couldn't go with people. I was a loner. . . . It took years after the war for me to realize that the Earth is beautiful, not always ugly. Because I had so many friends killed in front of me, on the side of me, and how they missed me, I have no idea."

Vietnam veterans—who, like World War II veterans, were a mix of volunteers and draftees and probably expected, at least at the beginning of the war, a similar beatification—had the opposite problem. In *Recovering from the War*, Patience H. C. Mason relates her husband's story: "Bob, who never fired a gun in Vietnam . . . who saved hundreds of lives by going in for wounded when it was too hot for the medevacs . . . got off the plane to buy some magazines in Hawaii. The clerk smiled at him and asked if he was coming back from Vietnam. He smiled back and nodded. 'Murderer!' she said."

Compared with that kind of reception, the earnest pity that Iraq and Afghanistan veterans often receive is awkward to complain about. It can sometimes even work to our advantage. When a friend of mine went apartment hunting recently, he had a potential landlord cry and call him a "poor soul" because of his service. "I went along with it," he said sheepishly. He didn't want to blow his chances on the application.

Still, there is something deeply unsettling about the way we so often choose to think about those who served. "People only want to ask me about the worst things that happened," an Afghanistan veteran recently told me. "Never my best times in the Corps. Who were my favorite people I served with? Or even, hell, what was the biggest barracks rat I ever saw? It wasn't all bad."

The theologian Jonathan Edwards didn't consider pity an expression of "true virtue." Pity addresses the perceived suffering, not the whole individual. "Men may pity others under exquisite torment," Edwards wrote, "when yet they would have been grieved if they had seen their prosperity."

Pity sidesteps complexity in favor of narratives that we're comfortable with, reducing the nuances of a person's experience to a sound bite. Thus the response of a New York partygoer who—after a friend explained that the proudest moment of his deployment to Iraq came when his soldiers were fired on and decided not to fire back—replied, "That must make the nightmares even worse."

This insistence on treating veterans as objects of pity plays out in our national dialogue as well, whether it is Bill Maher saying on his April 4 HBO show, "Anytime you send anyone to war, they come back a little crazy," or a *Washington Times* article about PTSD claiming that "roughly 2.6 million veterans who serve in Iraq and Afghanistan suffer from PTSD-type symptoms." That is roughly the total number of veterans who served, which suggests that the reporter thought there might be a 100 percent saturation rate of PTSD among veterans.

Expert estimates of the actual prevalence of PTSD vary between 11 percent and 20 percent for Iraq and Afghanistan veterans, according to the U.S. Veterans Administration. A 2012 VA report concluded that 247,243 veterans had been diagnosed with the disorder at VA hospitals and clinics. (For some perspective on these numbers: According to experts cited by the VA, some 8 percent of the overall U.S. population suffers from PTSD at some point in their lives, compared with up to 10 percent of Desert Storm veterans and about 30 percent of those from Vietnam.)

Some of these diagnosed veterans are my friends, and though their injuries certainly deserve all the research and support that we as a society can give, the current narrative about PTSD does them no favors. Even the Pulitzer Prize–winning reporter David Finkel, who has produced some of the bravest and most admirable reporting on the Iraq War and its aftermath, can fall into uncomfortable generalizations. In his recent book *Thank You for Your Service*, he writes of a battalion of eight hundred men: "All the soldiers . . . came home broken in various degrees, even the ones who are fine."

I don't know what it means to be simultaneously "broken" and "fine." I do have friends with real PTSD, which they manage with varying degrees of success. I also have friends whose pride in their service is matched by feelings of sorrow, anger, and bitterness. But I wouldn't classify them as "broken." If a friend of yours just died on his seventh deployment in a war that hardly makes the news anymore and you didn't feel sad, angry, and bitter, perhaps that is what counts as "broken." Likewise, if the absence of any public sense that we are a nation still at war doesn't leave you feeling alienated, perhaps that means you're "broken," too.

Pity places the focus on what's wrong with veterans. But for veterans looking at the society that sent them to war, it may not feel like they're the ones with the most serious problem.

Worse, those warm feelings of pity toward us broken veterans can too easily turn ugly. After the April 2 shooting spree at Fort Hood that left three soldiers dead and sixteen wounded, *The Huffington Post* ran an article titled "This Map Shows the Deadly Aftermath of War Right Here at Home," complete with a graphic showing killings committed by veterans.

Such "ticking-time-bomb" articles usually fail to put their numbers in perspective. Indeed, one Marine who had trained as an intelligence analyst crunched the murder-rate numbers for a VA blog and found that, if *The Huffington Post*'s numbers were accurate, the rate for veteran-committed homicide would still be a fourth of that for the general population. (*The Huffington Post* later took down the article, admitting that it was "incomplete and misleading.") While the exact numbers are difficult to measure, it appears that the crime rate for veterans is comparable to, if not lower than, the civilian crime rate, with veterans actually underrepresented in the U.S. prison population, according to Justice Department statistics.

As Sergeant Dakota Meyer, a young Marine and PTSD sufferer who was awarded the Medal of Honor for heroism in Afghanistan, explained after the Fort Hood shooting, "PTSD does not put you in the mind-set to go out and kill innocent people. . . . The media label this shooting PTSD, but if what that man did is PTSD, then I don't have it."

Kristen Rouse, a veteran and blogger who was struck by another article alerting fearful readers to zip codes that have large numbers of veterans with PTSD, wrote that the article treated a PTSD database "like a sex offender registry." A recent opinion piece in *The New York Times* even tried to link combat trauma with membership in the Ku Klux Klan. If vets are truly "broken," after all, there really is no telling what they might do.

This perspective is more than a little bizarre. Veterans rank among our most engaged, productive citizens. Just look at nonprofit groups such as The Mission Continues, which provides public-service fellowships for veterans across the country ("Reporting for duty in your community," their website says), or at the engagement efforts of groups such as the Iraq and Afghanistan Veterans of America (which strives to connect "the 99% of the population who haven't served in Iraq or Afghanistan with the 1% who have").

In New York, the contributions being made by veterans couldn't have been more apparent than after Hurricane Sandy. When the city failed to coordinate relief efforts in the Rockaways, the veteran-led relief group Team Rubicon filled the leadership gap by using a data-visualization program called Palantir to map conditions and coordinate efforts to help people stranded after the storm. Veterans are used to creating order in chaotic environments—just the sort of people a city in a crisis needs.

But let's not see the veterans engaged in this work as a group of "healthy" veterans who can be contrasted easily with a second group of "broken" veterans. Some of our most inspiring veterans have been plagued by the same issues that tend to receive such hyperbolic press. One of the founders of Team Rubicon, Clay Hunt, was a Marine who served two deployments in Iraq, provided relief efforts after earthquakes in Chile and Haiti, raised money for wounded veterans, and helped lobby Congress for veterans' benefits. He also, at age twenty-eight, joined the sad ranks of veterans who have taken their own lives.

I suppose that pity is one natural response to such a story. But I find it difficult to pity someone who, when his life is considered in its totality, achieved so much good and touched so many people.

War subjects some of its participants to more than any person can bear, and it destroys them. War makes others stronger. For most of us, it leaves a complex legacy. And though many veterans appreciate the well-meaning sentiments behind even the most misdirected pity, I can't help feeling that all of us, especially those who are struggling, deserve a little less pity and a little more respect.

THE LESSON OF ERIC GREITENS, AND THE NAVY SEALS WHO TRIED TO WARN US

MAY 17, 2018

Author's note: On the one hand, the story of Eric Greitens, who has since left government in disgrace, is old news. But the manner in which Greitens successfully leveraged the symbolism of the military, first in the nonprofit world, and later in politics, is a case study in the peculiar relationship between the American public and the military they venerate but know little about. In that regard, we may look at Greitens as an especially skilled political entrepreneur whose manipulation of his public image says as much about us as it does about him.

The Missouri legislature is scheduled to begin a special session, on Friday, to discuss whether to impeach Eric Greitens, the state's embattled governor. A former Navy SEAL who was once a rising star in the Republican Party, Greitens is now fighting allegations of sexual coercion, blackmail, invasion of privacy, and misuse of charity resources to fund his campaign. The charges stunned many in Missouri, but in the tight-knit SEAL community, Greitens has been a divisive figure for years. In 2016, before Greitens was elected, a group of mostly anonymous current and former SEALs tried to sound the alarm about why they thought he was unfit for office. "What we were afraid of is that, eighteen months from now, you've got candidate Greitens, former Navy SEAL, running for president," Paul Holzer, a former SEAL who worked on the campaign of one of Greitens's gubernatorial primary opponents, John Brunner, told me. But Greitens, who used his military background to create a public image of honor, courage, and leadership, was largely able to deflect their criticism.

After the killing of Osama bin Laden by SEAL Team Six in a 2011 raid, Navy SEALs became full-blown celebrities, and Greitens rode that fame to speaking tours, a spot on *Time* magazine's 2013 "100 Most Influential People" list, and, eventually, the governor's mansion. The success of the raid also intensified a growing division in the SEAL community.

SEALs have traditionally embraced a culture of quiet professionalism. Part of the SEAL credo reads, "I do not advertise the nature of my work, nor seek recognition for my actions." In the last two weeks, I spoke to more than half a dozen current and former SEALs about the spectacular implosion of Greitens's public image. Most chose not to go on the record, but all expressed frustration that a peripheral and contentious figure in their community, one who served overseas but never served with SEALs in combat, became a public face of the SEAL community. Many complained to me that it tends to be those who are least representative of SEAL core values, such as Greitens, who end up trading on the group's reputation and representing it in public, earning respect from American citizens but contempt from other SEALs.

In 2015, Lieutenant Forrest S. Crowell, a Navy SEAL, wrote a thesis for Naval Postgraduate School titled "Navy SEALs Gone Wild." In it, he argued that the SEALs' celebrity status had diverted their culture "away from the traditional SEAL Ethos of quiet professionalism to a Market Ethos of commercialization and self-promotion." Crowell warned that the new approach incentivized "narcissistic and profit-oriented behavior" and undermined healthy civil-military relations by using "the credibility of special operations to push partisan politics."

Greitens, who has been in office for a year and a half, is accused of coercing his former hairdresser into a sexual encounter in 2015 and threatening her to keep her quiet. According to her testimony, he led her into his basement, bound her hands, blindfolded her, ripped off her clothes, took her photograph, and demanded she perform oral sex. He told her that if she made details of the encounter public, he would release the photograph. Greitens also faces felony charges for tampering with a computer to gain access to a donor list associated with the charity organization he founded in 2007. The allegations, which Greitens has denied, will be considered in the Missouri General Assembly special session. The revelations have provoked bipartisan condemnation, with several Missouri Republican state lawmakers sending a letter to Donald Trump asking him to demand that Greitens step down. The president has not responded.

GREITENS'S CONTROVERSIAL REPUTATION among the SEALs began, oddly, when he performed what could arguably be considered an act of integrity. In 2004, he was a junior officer in the Navy SEALs, taking part in a large military exercise in Thailand. While there, he suspected that the ranking SEAL officer in his squadron, a highly respected combat veteran named Scott Hobbs, might have been abusing and distributing drugs.

Greitens was new to the command and had yet to prove himself. "Culturally, you're not viewed as a SEAL until you've deployed in a SEAL platoon," one former operator told me. In Thailand, Greitens served in a unit that supported one of the deployed platoons, the "team guys," who were considered the force's rock stars. The exercise was a chance for Greitens to get command time and learn how the SEALs worked before getting assigned to a platoon and heading to Iraq or Afghanistan. For a few of the SEALs in Thailand, though, the exercise was a chance to unwind between combat tours with binge drinking, drugs, and prostitutes.

The easiest course of action for Greitens would have been to look the other way or report the problem to the senior enlisted officer in the unit, who likely would have addressed the issue in-house. But Greitens worried that some of his sailors were taking part in the drug use and reached up to senior leadership outside Thailand. Drug tests were ordered. "We have a rat," Hobbs told his men. Hobbs tested positive, along with four other SEALs, and three special-boats crewmen. Courts-martial were scheduled, and two SEAL platoons that had been preparing to deploy in Iraq or Afghanistan were sent home. SEAL platoons in Baghdad that had been expecting to be relieved had their tours extended. Other stateside platoons were deployed early and kept overseas for eight or more months. They were told that one individual was responsible for their extension—Eric Greitens.

Senior leadership approved of Greitens's decision to report the drug use, but others in the community believed he should have handled the issue within his local chain of command. (Greitens would later claim that the incident was an example of SEAL values winning out.) Greitens's time in Thailand would be his last significant deployment as a SEAL. When he came home, he was offered an assistant platoon commander billet, but he declined, a SEAL working in his unit at the time told me. It wasn't a command position in the SEALs, and Greitens had other opportunities lined up, including a prestigious White House Fellowship. He would instead deploy with a unit training and assisting Kenyan forces in Manda Bay, and then leave active duty.

"Greitens is extremely smart, and he had a timeline," one of his fellow officers told me. "Everything he has done, he's done thinking ten moves in advance." Greitens later deployed to Iraq as a reservist, in 2006, and suffered chlorine inhalation and other injuries after a suicide truck bombing, but he ended his time on active duty never having led SEALs in combat.

GREITENS'S POLITICAL RISE coincided with a period when the navy itself sanctioned, in a few well-known cases, the commercialization and politicization of Special Operations. In 2007, Marcus Luttrell's bestselling memoir, *Lone Survivor*, an account of a disastrous operation in Afghanistan, was published with the blessing of Naval Special Warfare Command, despite containing contentious factual claims regarding Saddam Hussein's connection to al-Qaeda, as well as overt political speech that criticized "liberals" and the "liberal media." A year later, the NSWC endorsed the film *Act of Valor*, which starred active-duty Navy SEALs and grossed $81 million. It was in this environment that Greitens wrote his own memoir, *The Heart and the Fist*.

Greitens's book opens with the story of the chlorine-gas attack in Iraq. "It felt as if someone had shoved an open-flame lighter inside my mouth," he wrote. He detailed his education as a Rhodes Scholar and his humanitarian work. Mother Teresa makes an appearance. In the epilogue, Greitens described a trip to visit wounded service members, where he realized that many of them didn't want charity so much as a chance to continue to serve their country. This inspired him to create his own highly regarded veterans' organization, The Mission Continues, which offers fellowships to help veterans do service work back in their communities.

The Heart and the Fist is a unique, often compelling book that was also blessed with good timing. It came out three weeks before Barack Obama announced the death of bin Laden, and interest in the Navy SEALs exploded. Again, political and military officials encouraged the interest. The CIA director at the time, Leon Panetta, revealed classified details regarding the raid at a ceremony attended by the screenwriter of *Zero Dark Thirty*. Vice President Joe Biden commented publicly on the SEALs' role in the operation. News organizations were eager to find veterans willing to offer themselves up as experts to explain the Navy SEALs to a captivated American audience. Greitens quickly obliged.

In the days and weeks after the raid, Greitens, who was still a navy reservist, discussed SEAL Team Six with *The Wall Street Journal*, NPR, *The Washington Post*, and MSNBC. He appeared on *The Colbert Report* and joked coyly about how a SEAL like him couldn't say whether he participated in the raid. During one awkward exchange on Chris Matthews's *Hardball*, Matthews asked Greitens whether the computer simulations of the raid that the program had put together looked authentic. Greitens, who had no more experience on SEAL raids than Matthews did, demurred before complimenting the quality, if not accuracy, of the graphics. By May 22, Greitens's book had shot up to number 9 on *The New York Times* bestseller list.

"The first sentence out of his mouth was always 'I'm a Navy SEAL,'" one former operator complained to me. He didn't slight Greitens's service, but it frustrated him that Greitens had crafted a public persona so heavily reliant on honor earned by other men. Some prominent veterans and senior members of the military praised Greitens. The former Joint Chiefs chairman General Richard Myers called him a "modern-day Renaissance man" with a vision that is "an inspiration to all." Bob Muller, a cofounder of Vietnam Veterans of America, called him "exactly the kind of citizen-warrior that America needs."

Greitens avoided telling outright lies about his service or engaging in the kind of political commentary that other SEALs embraced—from Fox News contributor Benjamin Smith calling Obama a Muslim to Carl Higbie's use of racist, sexist, anti-Muslim, and antigay remarks during his time as a right-wing radio host. Instead, Greitens delivered the sort of talks on leadership and service that made him a welcome speaker at the Harvard Center for Public Leadership. He was interviewed by Jon Stewart on *The Daily Show* and made an appearance on *Charlie Rose*. Meanwhile, other members of the SEAL community grumbled about him, but mostly kept their criticism private. One former ROTC commander at a public university recalled reaching out to fellow former SEALs after a representative approached him about inviting Greitens to talk to the cadets. They responded not with visceral disgust, the former ROTC commander recalled, but with light disdain, saying, "Nah, don't bring him. He's a cheeseball."

THE ANIMUS SOME SEALs FELT toward Greitens flared in 2015, after he resigned from his position at The Mission Continues and announced his candidacy in the Missouri Republican gubernatorial primary. The Greitens whom the SEALs knew had been a lifelong Democrat. He had even attended the 2008 Democratic National Convention with the former Missouri governor Bob Holden. Now he was running ads touting his conservative credentials and his SEALs background.

In one campaign ad, Greitens fires an assault rifle at a target that then explodes, and the words "Conservative. Navy SEAL" appear next to his face. His campaign also sought to raise money selling bumper stickers that read "ISIS Hunting Permit," bragging, "Liberals will go crazy when they see these." The way these gimmicks seemed to exaggerate Greitens's background as a SEAL frustrated some members of the community.

"The guys who are the reason the SEALs are so respected are the guys on the front lines," one former officer said. "Their families are suffering; sometimes they develop PTSD, or traumatic brain injuries." That Greitens launched his political career on the back of those types of sacrifices struck many SEALs as dishonest. "I was doing back-to-back deployments, sometimes only four months in between," one told me, "and this guy never showed up."

But many of Greitens's critics were still hesitant to go public with their concerns. As operators who valued the SEAL tradition of quiet professionalism, they felt that it would defy the same ethos that they were accusing Greitens of violating. In February 2016, a group of SEALs decided to anonymously release an attack video that laid out their criticisms of Greitens's record. The video earned little attention in Missouri, in part because of its focus on details that most voters did not understand, like the distinction between those who serve with SEAL teams in combat versus those who don't.

Greitens responded with a forceful video of his own, in which he accused the men behind the attack of being cowards. Incensed, Holzer and his fellow Navy SEAL Drago Dzieran appeared on Dana Loesch's radio show to complain about Greitens's use of SEAL iconography and to demand that he "run on his own record, not on the record of SEALs." In March of that year, sixteen former and active SEAL team members involved with the video spoke out against Greitens in *The Missouri Times*, again anonymously. It wasn't enough.

The SEALs who supported Greitens tended to be, like him, celebrities or public figures. Congressman Ryan Zinke, the current secretary of the interior and a former SEAL Team Six commander, called him "a highly decorated combat veteran with a proven record of leading from the front." Rob O'Neill, the SEAL Team Six operator who claims to have shot Osama bin Laden, praised Greitens as a "combat leader," spoke at his rallies, and offered signed versions of the ISIS bumper stickers in exchange for a hundred-dollar donation to the Greitens campaign.

SINCE THE INVESTIGATION into Greitens began five months ago, the governor has resisted calls for his resignation and denounced the charges against him as a "witch hunt . . . exactly like what's happening with the witch hunts in Washington, D.C."

Zinke and O'Neill are now silent about their support for Greitens, but 63 percent of Republicans in Missouri say that they still approve of the governor, suggesting that he may survive the scandals despite bipartisan calls for his resignation. "His SEAL training has taught him never to surrender, never to walk away from a fight," a letter from Missouri state senator Rob Schaaf reads. "He is trained to endure pain, and those watching can easily see that he is enduring a lot of it, and he seems unmoved by the pain his fellow Missourians are also enduring as a result." Nate Walker, a Republican representative in Missouri, was one of the first legislators to call for his resignation. "The political and personal perils surrounding Eric Greitens are disturbing, and as time passes they get more complicated and serious," he told me. "His total credibility is now in question."

On Monday, state prosecutors abruptly dropped the criminal invasion-of-privacy charges against Greitens that stemmed from the alleged photograph of his former hairdresser, but a special prosecutor may be named to pursue a different case. Greitens called the development a victory and vowed to fight efforts to impeach him during Friday's special legislative session.

The likelihood that the SEAL community will return to its quiet past is small. Even before the Greitens scandal, the avalanche of SEAL memoirs had become a well-worn joke. "US Navy Adds Intense Creative Writing Course to SEAL Training," the headline of an article from the Duffel Blog, a satirical website, reads. "The people of this nation should be suspicious of SEALs who speak too loudly about themselves," Forrest Crowell wrote. Greitens has underscored the usefulness of this advice.

"It's probably unrealistic to say that nobody is ever going to go out there and talk about anything," Jason Redman, a retired Navy SEAL, told me. "And the other end of that spectrum is wrapping yourself in the trident, and going on Fox News, and talking about anything and everything for a buck." Redman, who survived multiple gunshot wounds to the arms and face, thirty-seven surgeries, and more than a hundred and ninety hours under general anesthesia, does speak publicly about his background. However, he takes care to clear his public remarks and activities with SEAL headquarters and avoids partisan commentary.

"I think they need to educate guys. If you're going to talk, you need to make sure it doesn't create a negative—or, worst case, operational—impact on the SEAL teams," he told me. "And that's going to take time as they change the culture." As for Greitens, he said, "Not only is it a black eye for us but a black eye for the military."

THE WARRIOR AT THE MALL

APRIL 14, 2018

W e're at war while America is at the mall."

I'm not sure when I first heard this in Iraq, but even back in 2007 it was already a well-worn phrase, the logical counterpart to George W. Bush's arguing after the September 11 attacks that we must not let the terrorists frighten us to the point "where people don't shop."

Marines had probably started saying it as early as 2002. "We're at war while America is at the mall," some lance corporal muttered to another as they shivered against the winds rushing down the valleys in the Hindu Kush. "We're at war while America is at the mall," some prematurely embittered lieutenant told his platoon sergeant as they drove up to Nasiriyah in a light armored vehicle.

Whatever the case, when I heard it, it sounded right. Just enough truth mixed with self-aggrandizement to appeal to a man in his early twenties. Back home was shopping malls and strip clubs. Over here was death and violence and hope and despair. Back home was fast food and high-fructose corn syrup. Over here, we had bodies flooding the rivers of Iraq until people claimed it changed the taste of the fish. Back home they had aisles filled wall to wall with toothpaste, shaving cream, deodorant, and body spray. Over here, sweating under the desert sun, we smelled terrible. We were at war, they were at the mall.

The old phrase popped back into my head recently while I was shopping for baby onesies on Long Island—specifically, in the discount section on the second floor of the Buy Buy Baby. Yes, I was at the mall, and America was still at war.

There's something bizarre about being a veteran of a war that doesn't end, in a country that doesn't pay attention. At this point, I've been out of the military far longer than I was in, and the weight I place on the value of military life versus civilian life has shifted radically. On the one hand, I haven't lost my certainty that Americans *should* be paying more attention to our wars and that our lack of attention truly does cost lives.

"We've claimed war-weariness, or 'America First,' and turned a blind eye to the slaughter of five hundred thousand people and suffering of millions more," the former Marine Mackenzie Wolf pointed out in a March essay on America's unconscionable lack of action in Syria up to that point. On the other hand, I'm increasingly convinced that my youthful contempt for the civilians back home was not just misplaced, but obscene and, frankly, part of the problem.

After four U.S. soldiers assigned to the army's Third Special Forces Group were killed in an ambush in Niger, the American public had a lot of questions. Why were they in combat in Niger? What was their mission? How do you pronounce "Niger"? Answering these questions would have required a complex, sustained discussion about how America projects force around the world, about expanding the use of Special Operations forces to 149 countries, and about whether we are providing those troops with well-thought-out missions and the resources to achieve them in the service of a sound and worthwhile national security strategy.

And since our troops were in Niger in a continuation of an Obama administration policy that began in 2013, it also would have meant discussing the way that administration ramped up "supervise, train and assist" missions in Africa, how it often tried to blur the line between advisory and combat missions to avoid public scrutiny, and how the Trump administration appears to have followed in those footsteps. It would have required, at a bare minimum, not using the deaths as material for neat, partisan parables.

Naturally, we didn't have that conversation. Instead, a Democratic congresswoman who heard the president's phone call to the widow of one of the fallen soldiers informed the news media that Mr. Trump had ineptly told the grieving woman that her husband "knew what he signed up for."

Quickly, Americans shifted from a discussion of policy to a symbolic battle over which side, Democratic or Republican, wasn't respecting soldiers enough. Had the president disrespected the troops with his comment? Had Democrats disrespected the troops by trying to use a condolence call for political leverage? Someone clearly had run afoul of an odd form of political correctness, "patriotic correctness."

Since, as recent history has shown us, violating the rules of patriotic correctness is a far worse sin in the eyes of the American public than sending soldiers to die uselessly, the political battle became intense, and the White House was forced to respond. And since in a symbolic debate of this kind nothing is better than an old soldier, the retired Marine general and current chief of staff, John Kelly, was trotted out in an October 19 news conference to defend the president.

He began powerfully enough, describing what happens to the bodies of soldiers killed overseas, and bringing up his own still painful memories of the loss of his son, who died in Afghanistan in 2010. He spoke with pride of the men and women in uniform.

But then, in an all-too-common move, he transitioned to expressing contempt for the civilian world. He complained that nothing seemed to be sacred in America anymore, not women, not religion, not even "the dignity of life." He told the audience that service members volunteer even though "there's nothing in our country anymore that seems to suggest that selfless service to the nation is not only appropriate, but required." He said veterans feel "a little bit sorry" for civilians who don't know the joys of service.

To cap things off, he took questions only from reporters who knew families who had lost loved ones overseas. The rest of the journalists, and by extension the rest of the American public who don't know any Gold Star families, were effectively told they had no place in the debate.

Such disdain for those who haven't served and yet dare to have opinions about military matters is nothing new for Kelly. In a 2010 speech after the death of his son, Kelly improbably claimed that we were winning in Afghanistan, but that "you wouldn't know it because successes go unreported" by members of the "'know-it-all' chattering class" who "always seem to know better, but have never themselves been in the arena." And he argued that to oppose the war, which our current secretary of defense last year testified to Congress we were not winning, meant "slighting our warriors and mocking their commitment to the nation."

This is a common attitude among a significant faction of veterans. As one former member of the Special Forces put it in a social media post responding to the liberal outcry over the deaths in Niger, "We did what we did so that you can be free to naïvely judge us, complain about the manner in which we kept you safe" and "just all around live your worthless sponge lives." His commentary, which was liked and shared thousands of times, is just a more embittered form of the sentiment I indulged in as a young lieutenant in Iraq.

It can be comforting to reverse the feelings of hopelessness and futility that come with fighting seemingly interminable, strategically dubious wars by enforcing a hierarchy of citizenship that puts the veteran and those close to him on top, and everyone else far, far below.

But John Kelly's contempt for modern civilian life wasn't a pep talk voiced in a Humvee traveling down an Iraqi highway, or at a veterans' reunion in a local bar. He was speaking to the American people, with the authority of a retired general, on behalf of the president of the United States of America. And he was letting us know our place.

Those with questions about military policy are being put in their place more and more often these days. When reporters later asked the White House press secretary, Sarah Huckabee Sanders, about some of Kelly's claims, which had proved false, she said, "If you want to get into a debate with a four-star Marine general, I think that's highly inappropriate." It was an echo of the way Sean Spicer tried to short-circuit debate about the death of a Navy SEAL in Yemen by claiming that anyone who questioned the success of the raid "owes an apology" to the fallen SEAL.

Serious discussion of foreign policy and the military's role within it is often prohibited by this patriotic correctness. Yet, if I have authority to speak about our military policy it's because I'm a citizen responsible for participating in self-governance, not because I belonged to a warrior caste.

If what I say deserves to be taken seriously, it's because I've taken the time out of my worthless sponge life as a concerned American civilian to form a worthy opinion. Which means that although it is my patriotic duty to afford men like John Kelly respect for his service, and for the grief he has endured as the father of a son who died for our country, that is not where my responsibility as a citizen ends.

I must also assume that our military policy is of direct concern to me, personally. And if a military man tries to leverage the authority and respect he is afforded to voice contempt for a vast majority of Americans, if he tries to stifle their exercise of self-governance by telling them that to question the military strategy of our generals and our political leaders is a slight to our troops, it's my patriotic duty to tell him to go pound sand.

If we don't do this, we risk our country slipping further into the practice of a fraudulent form of American patriotism, where "soldiers" are sacred, the work of actual soldiering is ignored, and the pageantry of military worship sucks energy away from the obligations of citizenship.

I understand why politicians and writers and institutions choose to employ the trope of veterans when it comes to arguing for their causes. Support for our military remains high at a time when respect for almost every other institution is perilously low, so pushing a military angle as a wedge makes a certain kind of sense. But our peacetime institutions are not justified by how they intermittently intersect with national security concerns—it's the other way around. Our military is justified only by the civic life and values it exists to defend. This is why George Washington, in his Farewell Orders to the Continental Army, told his troops to "carry with them into civil society the most conciliating dispositions" and "prove themselves not less virtuous and useful as citizens than they have been persevering and victorious as soldiers."

Besides, let's not pretend that living a civilian life—and living it *well*—isn't hard. A friend of mine, an officer in the Army Reserves, told me that one of his greatest leadership challenges came not overseas, but when a deployment to Afghanistan got canceled and his men were called to the difficult and often tedious work of being husbands, fathers, members of a community.

My wife and I are raising two sons—the older one is two years old, the little one six months. And as we follow our national politics with occasional disgust, amusement, horror, and hope, we regularly talk about the sort of qualities we want to impress upon our boys so they can be good citizens, and how we can help cultivate in them a sense of service, of gratitude for the blessings they have, and a desire to give back. It's a daunting responsibility. Right now, though, the day-to-day work of raising these kids doesn't involve a lot of lofty rhetoric about service. It involves drool, diapers, and doing the laundry. For me, it means being that most remarkable, and somehow most unremarkable, of things—a dad.

Which is how I found myself that day, less a Marine veteran than a father, shopping with the other parents at Buy Buy Baby, recalling that old saying, "We're at war while America is at the mall." I wondered about the anonymous grunt poet who coined it. Whoever he was, there's a good chance that even by the time I heard it, he'd already done his four years and gotten out.

Maybe he'd left the Corps, settled into civilian life. Maybe he was in school. Perhaps he was working as a schoolteacher, or as a much-derided civil servant in some corner of our government. Perhaps he found that work more satisfying, more hopeful, and of more obvious benefit to his country than the work he'd done in our mismanaged wars.

Or perhaps, if he was as lucky as I have been, he was in some other mall doing exactly what I was—trying to figure out the difference between 6M and 3-6M baby onesies. If so, I wish him well.

THE SOLDIERS WE LEAVE BEHIND

WAR, IMMIGRATION, AND WHAT IT MEANS
TO BE AN AMERICAN

NOVEMBER 9, 2019

W e're Americans!" Ali shouted as bullets shattered the glass of the car he hid behind. "Americans!"

He'd been fighting alongside U.S. troops for years by then. He'd faced IED-riddled streets and served in the 2004 battle of Najaf, one of the fiercest early battles of the Iraq War. But never before had he been so certain he was going to die.

Ali's lieutenant was wounded in the shoulder. Reinforcements were an hour away. And it seemed as though the whole city of Baghdad were shooting at them.

This was in 2006, in a neighborhood called Hurriya, as sectarian violence was beginning to engulf Iraq. Two days before, Shiites from the Ministry of the Interior had showed up and taken away several youths for "questioning," only to execute them and dump their bodies in the street. And then Ali arrived with a newly trained Iraqi Special Forces unit and three American soldiers.

"We hit the town," he later explained, "and the target's family took a shot at us, thinking that this is the same people who came two days ago." They fired back, and soon gunfire was coming from all around. Which is when Ali started trying to calm things by announcing that they were Americans.

But Ali himself wasn't American—at least not yet. Born in Baghdad, the son of an Iraqi Army sergeant major, he'd come to hold ideas about America that by 2006, after years of occupation that included prisoner abuse at Abu Ghraib and the Haditha killings of unarmed civilians, many of his fellow Iraqis didn't share.

Those ideas were forged when Ali was a thirteen-year-old awaiting the Persian Gulf War. Rumors spread that Americans would defile Iraq's holy places, pervert the culture, and torture the innocent. "We didn't know anything," Ali said. "We were living in a big prison." Ali's father noticed his family's nervousness and gathered the clan together. "Americans would never target civilians," he told them. "So let's just enjoy the show."

It took the September 11 attacks to bring "the show." Once again, rumors swirled: The Humvee is indestructible. American soldiers take one pill and they don't eat or drink for days. And then came first contact. Thousands of leaflets raining from the sky, delivering the message: "The Coalition wishes no harm to the innocent Iraqi civilians." To Ali, it confirmed his father's belief in the difference between America and the brutal Saddam Hussein regime his whole family hated but never talked about. "I took one of the leaflets and showed my father," Ali said, "and he was like, 'Yeah, I told you, man.'"

And so Ali signed up as an interpreter for the Americans, whose official rhetoric claimed they were promoting classical liberal values in Iraq, establishing a vision realized on their own shores but belonging to all mankind—democracy, freedom, and equality. At least that was the theory. And in theory, we could "go forward with complete confidence," as President George W. Bush proclaimed, "because freedom is the permanent hope of mankind, the hunger in dark places, the longing of the soul." In theory, that longing would lead Iraqis to greet American troops as liberators and make the shouted words "We're Americans!" capable of calming a firefight in a hostile neighborhood.

In practice, and in American history, more has been required. America may be "a nation of immigrants," where people of different nations and faiths forge a common identity. But that common identity has relied on far more than the notion of all people hungering for freedom in dark places. For citizens to labor and sacrifice on a nation's behalf, they must feel what Edward Wilmot Blyden called "the poetry of politics," that sense of inclusion in a broader community with its own distinctive character and historical consciousness.

The American problem was reconciling this with a universalistic ethic open to all people. And throughout our history, we have relied not simply on ideas but on a far more atavistic, unstable, and dangerous tool: war.

DURING THE 1912 PRESIDENTIAL ELECTION, Charles White Whittlesey, the man who would arguably become the greatest hero of World War I—a man so famous that even the carrier pigeon who delivered his battlefield messages became a household name—cast his vote for the pacifist socialist Eugene Debs. Whittlesey, a tall, bookish, twenty-eight-year-old lawyer, had taken to socialism as a student a decade earlier at Williams College. In the words of the historian Robert J. Laplander, he believed "socialism could be the only vehicle through which a wider cooperation of peoples of all types could come about."

That was a pressing issue in 1912. Great waves of new immigrants had come to America starting in the 1880s, immigrants the United States Immigration Commission declared were "races" deficient in "intelligence, manliness, cooperation," and other qualities without which "democracy is futile." About a third of the nation was foreign born or the child of a foreign-born parent. One-tenth was black.

But the outbreak of a European Great War meant these derided groups could prove their Americanness on the battlefield. When immigrants and native-born Americans rub "elbows in a common service to a common Fatherland," claimed the assistant secretary of war, Henry Breckinridge, "out comes the hyphen—up goes the Stars and Stripes. . . . Universal military service will be the elder brother of the public school in fusing this American race."

There were less martial versions of this idea. After a German submarine had torpedoed a British liner and killed 128 Americans, Woodrow Wilson even suggested to a crowd of 4,000 newly naturalized citizens, many from Germany, that it was immigrants themselves who helped define Americanness. "A man does not go out to seek the thing that is not in him," he said, and "if some of us have forgotten what America believed in, you, at any rate, imported in your own hearts a renewal of the belief."

Whittlesey assumed America would enter the war and that every honorable American should serve. Disillusioned with the Socialist Party's pacifism, he entered military training in 1916. When the United States entered the war in 1917, he was assigned to one of the new regiments being formed in that most suspicious of places—New York.

"Patriots" had warned against raising troops there. New York was filled with blacks and immigrants, as the new regiments would reflect. The 369th "Harlem Hellfighters" were a black American infantry regiment whose service, civil rights activists like James Weldon

Johnson believed, would help ensure "the right to claim the full rights of citizenship." And then there was the 308th Infantry, part of the "Melting Pot Division" and heavily weighted with Italians, Eastern Europeans, Chinese, and Jews. As one soon-to-be highly decorated soldier from another division that would train and fight alongside those men, Alvin York, described in his diary, "They put me by some Greeks and Italians to sleep. I couldn't understand them and they couldn't understand me." It was in the 308th that Whittlesey would fight.

Whittlesey's unit saw initial action in Alsace-Lorraine and acquitted itself well. In his diary York noted, "Those Greeks and Italians and New York Jews were sure turning out to be good soldiers." And then, in late September in the Meuse-Argonne, they would earn their fame.

"Let's go!" Whittlesey rasped, striding toward the Argonne Forest, over what one officer described as a "blind world of whiteness and noise, groping over something like the surface of the moon." It was the first of several pushes over several days. Communication lines kept getting cut. Their left flank became increasingly exposed, a concern Whittlesey's senior officer waved off as "nonsense." On October 2, Whittlesey led a further attack. It did not go well.

They lost contact with flanking units and were completely encircled by the most experienced Germans, as recounted by Jonathan H. Ebel in *G.I. Messiahs*. They shot American runners and repeatedly assaulted the unit. Whittlesey's battalion had low supplies, then no supplies. They had to strip bandages off corpses to apply to the freshly wounded. Whittlesey kept calm, buried his dead, and refused demands for surrender. For five days.

His men died in scores. And their death cries wouldn't have been only in English. Of the total American Expeditionary Force sent over to Europe, nearly a quarter were foreign born, speaking 49 languages. When friendly units reached Whittlesey, some 360 of his 554 men were dead, missing, or injured. The survivors became instant heroes.

"The Forest of Argonne blazed all at once into russets and golds and purples," wrote one reporter, "and here and there a scarlet tree, as though the roots had drunk deep of young American blood spent freely for an eternal cause once more defended on those hills." But how, precisely, to define that "eternal cause"?

When President Wilson asked Congress to declare war, he claimed he simply wished to champion "the rights of mankind." For Whittlesey, who would endorse the League of Nations, universalist idealism clearly resonated. For the rest of the country, though, it was a harder sell.

Wartime paranoia provided fodder for nativists who'd always despised those who, as the New York police commissioner put it in 1906, "can't talk the English language" and "are in general the scum of Europe."

So when Whittlesey delivered a speech in New York a mere two months after surviving the Argonne, he found himself out of step with his country. After recounting the heroism of the battalion's Catholic chaplain, James Halligan, Whittlesey informed the audience, "Our men who have been facing and fighting the Germans won't come back hating them. Why, they might even share their cigarettes with the Kaiser himself if they met him on the road." One newspaper account noted, "Silence greeted this portion of the speaker's address."

IN 2007, a spiky-haired kid who went by the name Ted signed up for the same job Ali had taken in 2004—interpreter for U.S. forces.

Originally from northern Iraq, Ted had learned English watching shows like *Cheers* and *Seinfeld*. To him, America was Soup Nazis and bars where everyone knew your name. And like Ali, he welcomed the coming invasion.

But when insurgents threatened him for talking to Americans, he'd fled to Syria for a year. This meant Ted, who picked his interpreter name because of a fondness for the actor Ted Danson, began working with Marines at a different—and very deadly—stage of the war. His first posting was with a Marine reconnaissance unit.

"I had no idea what Marine recon was," he recalled, laughing. Ted, with barely any training but attached to an aggressive, elite unit, soon found himself under fire. "I got a cold feeling," he said. "I didn't feel anything." But this numbness helped him operate, as did the example of the Marines around him. "It's very intense, firefights," he said. "But the people I worked with, they're brave men."

Ted soon proved his own bravery. During a platoonwide operation, his unit exchanged fire with insurgents, one of whom signaled he'd like to surrender. Since captured insurgents could yield critical, time-sensitive intelligence, Ted ran through enemy fire to the house and conducted an interrogation that, according to the commendation written by his battalion commander, helped "decisively end the engagement."

Around this time Ted learned of a new program offering special immigrant visas to those who worked with U.S. armed forces. In one sense, the program could be seen as a smaller-scale continuation of that old American idea that you could earn the title "American" by fighting for America.

But the program had a second, more practical purpose: to prove that America was a trustworthy partner in the complex wars we're currently fighting. Interpreters are essential links between American soldiers and the local troops they train, the neighborhoods they patrol, and the intelligence sources they depend on.

To insurgent groups, cutting off the link is critical. "Nine bullets for the apostate, one for the Crusader," was the slogan of an early ISIS strategy, emphasizing killing Muslim allies over Americans. That is why they have gunned down interpreters, kidnapped and beheaded them, killed their cousins and fathers and friends. And it is why generals like David Petraeus and Stanley McChrystal have publicly supported the program. One of the early beneficiaries was none other than Ali.

In 2007, one year after that firefight in Hurriya, Ali received a visa for the United States. Within a year, he joined the United States Army. His own trajectory seemed proof that the American dream was alive and well and truly universal.

For Ted, though, the American dream would prove harder to reach. He'd started fighting with Americans later in the war, and so by the time he would apply, events in both Iraq and America would make following Ali's path far more difficult.

First, his career as an interpreter ended with an on-the-job back injury that left him lying in a bed for months without support or medication. Then, as ISIS began taking territory, the State Department removed nonessential staff and discontinued refugee processing for six months. Since security clearances have an expiration date, this created a cascade effect, where applicants who had been cleared had to redo their screening process, all during a time when there were fewer personnel to conduct interviews and applications were spiking because everyone who had worked with Americans was under increased threat.

"He's like a Marine to me," said the former Marine Ben Wormington, who fought alongside Ted. "A Marine that we've left behind. If they stamped his passport, I would pay for his flight and his family would live in my house in Omaha."

Nevertheless, his case languished in the backlog. And then Donald Trump became president, a man who had called for a shutdown of Muslim immigration and suggested that the children of Muslim American parents were responsible for terrorist attacks, that Arab Americans had cheered the September 11 attacks, that for Muslims there is "no real assimilation." Once again, as occurred a century before, the fitness of a category of people for American democracy was called into question, and the immigration system would soon respond.

At first, admissions moved only slightly more slowly, with 11,929 total admissions of Iraqi refugees and special immigrants in fiscal year 2016, and 9,341 in 2017. In January 2017, the travel ban hit, suspending refugee admissions to the United States for 120 days. And though the administration would eventually clarify that the ban affected only one of the two main programs used by interpreters, the pace nonetheless slowed considerably. By fiscal year 2018, there would be only 745 admissions. By 2019, 646.

This prompted a March 8 letter from thirty-two members of Congress of both parties complaining about the administration's slow processing of visas. "The Iraqi program has a backlog of more than 100,000 people due to slowdowns," the letter noted. This echoed earlier complaints from the Pentagon that the delays would harm national security.

They have also harmed Ted. He lives under threat, in an area of Iraq controlled by militias. Not even his children know about his past, because a slip of the tongue could mean his life. The execution of a former interpreter, after all, is a powerful propaganda tool. It would suggest that America doesn't live up to its promises or keep faith with those who served it. But of course, this would hardly be the first time, or the last, that America has betrayed those who fought for it.

By 1919, after the conclusion of the war that had claimed 116,516 American lives, President Wilson's message about foreign-born Americans had changed. "Any man who carries a hyphen about with him carries a dagger that he is ready to plunge into the vitals of this Republic whenever he gets ready," he said. Many of those 116,516 were carrying hyphens.

The Socialist Party's 1917 response to American entry into the war said that wars "breed a sinister spirit of passion, unreason, race hatred and false patriotism," and the following years provided ample proof.

There had already been anti-immigrant violence, like the lynching of a German-born man, Robert Paul Prager. Meanwhile, groups like the Ku Klux Klan, the American Protective Association, and the Native Sons of the Golden West intimidated and scrutinized German, Catholic, Jewish, and Japanese immigrants.

As is usual in American history, though, the violence fell heaviest on black Americans. They came home from war to a wave of anti-black riots. And black veterans quickly found their service acknowledged not as a claim to full citizenship but as a threat. The attacks on them included lynchings, many detailed in the work of the historian Vincent Mikkelsen.

There was Private Charles Lewis, arrested while in uniform, beaten by a mob, lynched and left swinging from a blood-soaked rope on December 15, 1918, little more than a month after the armistice.

Wilbur Little, arrested for wearing his military uniform for "too long," was beaten to death in Blakely, Georgia.

Bud Johnson, chained to a stake in Pace, Florida, was reported to have said, "Would that I had died in Germany rather than come back here and die by the hand of the people I was protecting," then burned alive.

More followed. Frank Livingston. Robert Truett. Charles Kelly. Clinton Briggs. Jim Grant. Lucius McCarty and others. Veterans of the Great War were hung from telephone poles and bridges, dragged behind cars, burned, beaten, chained to trees, and riddled with bullets.

In postwar America only certain versions of self-sacrifice began to count. They were those that could be interpreted as sacrifice on behalf of a very particular, racially, ethnically, and culturally defined version of Americanness.

That's why a 1919 Armistice Day parade could end with the lynching of Wesley Everest, a veteran who was a member of the Industrial Workers of the World. And the Emergency Quota Act of 1921, which imposed the first numerical limits on immigration, passed in the same year as the interment of the Unknown Soldier, when the president and congressmen and Supreme Court justices and tens of thousands of Americans paid homage to a corpse made unrecognizable by war. The corpse was marched down the National Mall; a quartet of singers from the Metropolitan Opera compared his sacrifice to Christ's. And one of the pallbearers was Charles White Whittlesey.

No doubt, most of the mourners imagined a strapping, young, white, native-born American in the coffin, but he was chosen from corpses ravaged beyond recognition by war. He could have been anyone.

He could even have been from Whittlesey's battalion. And Whittlesey would have been acutely aware of the disconnect between the glorious celebration for this unknown soldier and the lives his men faced back here in America.

In his years home, Whittlesey became more guarded, though he did speak out against discrimination, claiming at an event organized to protest anti-Semitism, "If I am ever pessimistic of the future of this country, I would always feel assured that I could go to the crowded quarters of the city and pick out Herschkowitz, Ciriglio and O'Brien, and know that in them I could find the kind of men that were needed." He helped the Polish stowaway cousin of one of his soldiers avoid deportation. And the over-the-top ceremony for the Unknown Soldier deeply unsettled him. "I should not have come here," he told a friend. "I shall have nightmares tonight and hear the wounded screaming once again."

Soon after, Whittlesey visited friends. He organized his desk. He drew up a new will. Then, on November 26, he boarded a ship bound for Havana and during the night jumped from the deck and disappeared beneath the waters.

The story of Whittlesey's end has recently been recast as one of trauma or survivor's guilt. But in the immediate aftermath, there were other, less safely individualistic interpretations. To Willa Cather, whose cousin died in action in 1918, the war dead had a certain perverse luck. A man who died overseas could do so, she wrote in her novel *One of Ours*, "believing his own country better than it is." Those who lived, after all, had to face "the desolating disappointment" of postwar America. Too many of "the heroes of that war, the men of dazzling soldiership," would die by their own hand, like the one who chose to "slip over a vessel's side and disappear into the sea." She believed these suicides represented "the ones who had hoped extravagantly—who in order to do what they did had to hope extravagantly, and to believe passionately. And they found they had hoped and believed too much."

Ali acquitted himself well as a soldier, serving with Special Operations troops and playing an instrumental role in the capture of a high-level ISIS leader. He lives in Florida these days, still works in national security, and remains certain that his work allows him to fully live two identities, a hyphenated American providing a "service for America and for Iraq."

Ted waits for progress on his case. "When I've been in a bad situation," he says, "I'll imagine myself wearing my vest and my helmet, surrounded by Marines, and I'll tell myself, 'Hey, Ted, you're a Marine, you can get through these obstacles.' And that's why I'm still hanging in there, man."

Recent protests in Iraq have blacked out internet access, so Ben Wormington, the former Marine who served with Ted, checks Ted's email for him, so that he can call him if any word from the State Department ever comes. Wormington thinks supporting his brother-in-arms is just an extension of what it means to be a Marine and to serve his country. "Being an American is like being a Christian," he says. "It ain't easy. Nobody said it was going to be easy. But if you don't pursue those beliefs, then you don't believe."

Over Skype, Ted details some of the challenges he has been facing, including a recent bout of typhoid. "We got a lot of bad bugs here," he says with a grin, waving away his health issues. And then he turns ruminative.

"I want to live American dreams," he says. "To live free. Freedom and respect. That's the American dream. And I still think I'm a Marine. I'm honored to be a Marine. I wish that I could work with the Marines one more time." As he says this his children enter the room, and they come over and crawl over him. He smiles and laughs and adds: "I think I've got a chance. I did my interview. Just medical, and then I'm out of here."

Given the current state of our immigration and refugee policies, it's unlikely to be that easy. Nor is it quite clear, at a time when even those who literally risked their lives under fire for America are not allowed to come and add their skills and talents to the country, what precisely the "American dream" now means.

"It's about courage and cowardice," says Travis Weiner, a two-tour army infantry veteran whose interpreter was killed in Iraq years after he'd applied for a visa. "If people's emotions about immigration are such that they are willing to tolerate literally leaving our wartime allies behind on the battlefield because they're foreigners and they look different, even though they've done more for this country than most Americans—if that's the case, then we really need to do a gut check about whether we really are the people we say we are."

But as our recent abrupt withdrawal from Syria shows, where Kurds who fought with us have faced slaughter at Turkey's hands, leaving our battlefield allies behind is becoming a pattern. So what hope does that leave a guy like Ted?

Perhaps the story we tell ourselves is a lie. Perhaps there is another sort of distinct "Americanness." It's one thing to admit a Muslim refugee fleeing violence. But someone who has already fought and sacrificed for America, who has served in combat alongside elite military units in a time when only a fraction of Americans serve at all, is a much greater threat—not to our national security, but to that sense of ourselves and our "Americanness" that rears up in times of war.

Or perhaps our history offers other versions of American identity. By the end of his presidency, Ronald Reagan spoke of America as the city on a hill, a city "teeming with people of all kinds living in harmony and peace," where "if there had to be city walls, the walls had doors and the doors were open to anyone with the will and the heart to get here." In this vision, patriotism is tied to immigration. And it's a vision that corresponded to a continuing American reality.

America is home to 19 percent of the world's migrants, many times more than present in any other nation. Seventy-five percent of

Americans say immigration is a good thing, and 68 percent say openness to foreigners is "essential to who we are as a nation."

If that's true, then it means that part of the American character, our essential "Americanness," must lie in the very turbulence caused by immigration, the melding of different peoples as well as the new forms of cultural expression and patriotic commitment that arise in the process. In that regard, American identity is like Heraclitus's river, which no one can step into twice.

But to accept this requires faith in the fundamental principles of American life to unify diverse peoples. It requires a love of country, a bitter rage at how far we are from our country's promise, and a determination to work to make that promise a reality. More than anything, it requires a degree of optimism in the face of ceaseless change. It takes courage.

A HISTORY OF VIOLENCE

HOW FIREARMS HAVE GROWN MORE DEADLY,

ONE INNOVATION AT A TIME

America's first recorded murderer arrived on the *Mayflower*, and his weapon of choice was a gun. His name was John Billington, and to the leaders of the Plymouth Colony he was a troublemaker, from a family of troublemakers. Before arriving in America, Billington's son had already nearly blown up the *Mayflower* by firing off a gun near a barrel of gunpowder. On shore, Billington had run afoul of the law for "opprobrious speeches" in contempt of lawful commands, been implicated in a failed revolt against the Plymouth Church, and then, finally, in 1630, came the act that would send him to the gallows.

He'd gone out to the woods armed for deer. Instead, he came upon a man named John Newcomen. We don't know the nature of their disagreement. Billington had many grievances, some justified. He wasn't a religious separatist but a Church of Englander driven to colonization by poverty, and only by chance ended up with the Pilgrims, a severe group even other Puritans described as "a waspish, discontented people." The Pilgrims called Billington's family "one of the profanest" at Plymouth, and when they divided up the settlement, his family received the smallest per capita allotment of land, despite having been at the colony from its beginning. And yet he clearly had his supporters among those who chafed under the restrictive Puritan leadership. One critic of the colony described Billington as "beloved of many," and when they left, several defectors bequeathed their garden plots to him. It's easy to imagine Billington as a quintessentially American type: rebellious, freethinking, and murderous.

John Newcomen saw Billington coming and fled into the shelter of nearby trees as Billington took aim. It wasn't a terrible plan. Firearms of that era were rudimentary, slow, inaccurate, and prone to misfires. "Their bullets doo worke as much effect against the Moone, as against the Enemie that they shoote at," one pro-longbow military pamphlet argued. Had Billington missed or misfired, Newcomen could have escaped. In that era, reloading a firearm meant dropping it from the shoulder, pointing the muzzle upward, pouring in gunpowder, shoving in a bullet alongside a small piece of cloth, pushing both down the barrel with a ramrod until the bullet was seated against the powder charge, and then priming the firing mechanism. If the weapon had a cutting-edge flintlock ignition system, the shooter would then need to half-cock the hammer of his weapon, open a little pan sitting on top of the rifle, pour in gunpowder, close the pan, set the hammer to full cock, and only then take aim. If his rifle had a less advanced matchlock ignition, a total of twenty-eight steps would be required before he got another shot at killing his enemy. That'd provide plenty of time for Newcomen to flee.

But Billington didn't miss. His bullet struck Newcomen in the shoulder, crushing through tissues and, perhaps, crashing into bone and sending it shrapneling through his body. Newcomen died soon thereafter. Billington was tried, found guilty, and sentenced to death by hanging. In his journal, William Bradford, the governor of Massachusetts, noted that the hanging was carried out so that "the land be purged of blood."

Obviously, the purge didn't work. In 2017, Americans committed 19,510 homicides, 14,542 of which were carried out with firearms. Add in suicides, and 40,000 lives were ended by guns that year. Such numbers would have been inconceivable with colonial weaponry. Compared to the firearm, the historian Thomas McDade wrote, "the ax would appear to have been no less lethal a weapon in the eighteenth and nineteenth centuries." An ax, after all, does not require reloading with each use. But neither do the firearms of today. Modern guns are not just a different animal from the weapon that John Billington used to murder John Newcomen; they're a different species, belonging to a different genus, perhaps a different kingdom.

In 1630, John Billington had only one shot at ending John Newcomen's life. In 2017, a 64-year-old man devoid of advanced marksmanship skills or military training unloaded over 1,100 rounds on a crowd in Las Vegas over the course of 10 minutes, killing 58 people and wounding 422. In the wake of the shooting there were no calls to purge the land of blood. "New laws won't stop a madman," claimed President Trump, before announcing his intention to expand mental health facilities across the country, so that they could "take mentally deranged and dangerous people off of the streets." But the story of how we got from one bullet to 1,100 isn't a story of malfunctioning brains. It's a story of technological progress—of advances in chemistry, metallurgy, physics, medical science, and marketing. It is a story of ceaseless innovation.

I. THE BEATEN ZONE

Samuel Walker and his fellow Texas Rangers were supposed to be hunting Comanches. But the armed horsemen who appeared to their rear in June 1844, shouting taunts in Spanish, didn't look like prey. Walker had fifteen men. There were twenty Comanches visible, with more almost certainly hidden nearby.

The Comanches had been the dominant military power in the Southwest for over a century. Aggressive and imperial, the so-called Lords of the South Plains had shoved aside Apache and other Native American nations; raided colonial outposts in New Mexico, Texas, Louisiana, and northern Mexico; taken slaves; extracted tribute; and protected their economic interests through violence. The Comanche story, the historian Pekka Hämäläinen has written, reversed the usual historical roles: it was one "in which Indians expand, dictate, and prosper, and European colonists resist, retreat, and struggle to survive."

Each Ranger had a rifle—their standard weapon. That day, though, each man also carried a pair of Colt Paterson revolvers. The revolvers were new and mostly untested. Each gun had a revolving cylinder aligned against a stationary barrel. Drawing back the hammer would rotate the cylinder, setting one of five chambers in position to fire. All the shooter had to do was pull the trigger: there was no need to reload until all five rounds had been expended.

The Rangers understood, intellectually, how the revolvers worked. Still, they were slight, unimpressive-looking, and extremely inaccurate at range, and so they started by using their rifles. Rifles were a significant advance on the smoothbore musket Billington would have fired, with grooved barrels that imparted spin to their bullets, stabilizing them in flight and improving accuracy. But they didn't make so much a difference here. The Comanches rode back and forth, trying to goad the Rangers into taking shots. As the Rangers maneuvered away from the woods and around a slight hill, however, it became clear that they were outnumbered four to one. They attempted a series of rushes, including a daring rear assault into the Indian line, but eventually ran out of rifle ammo. The Comanches moved in for the kill.

As the Comanches rushed across the prairie, the men drew their pistols. When they closed in, the Rangers fired a volley. And then, without pause, another volley, and another, as the Comanches tumbled from their saddles. The Rangers "had a shot for every finger on the hand," a Comanche survivor later complained. The assaulting force fled, and the Rangers followed with counterattacks. (During one of these, Walker was speared from behind; a fellow Ranger shot Walker's attacker in the head and pulled Walker into a thicket, saving his life.) By the end of the day, the sixteen Rangers had killed twenty Comanches and wounded another thirty—most of the damage done with their Colts. "Up to this time, these daring Indians had always supposed themselves superior to us, man to man, on horse," Sam Walker later wrote. "The result of this engagement was such as to intimidate them and enable us to treat with them." For Rangers like Walker, this promised the decline of the Comanche empire and the increasing security of Texas as a burgeoning slave state.

AFTER THE BATTLE, Walker wrote to Samuel Colt, the inventor of the revolver, only to find that Colt had gone out of business, his Patent Fire-Arms Manufacturing Company in receivership. Demand for repeating firearms was low, and the gun industry as a whole was not robust. Ever since Eli Whitney had helped kick-start the American system of manufacturing in 1798 when he secured an order for ten thousand muskets and bayonets made with interchangeable parts, gun sellers had relied heavily on government contracts.

But generals awarded those contracts, and throughout American history generals have tended to focus on the accuracy of firearms, while undervaluing rate of fire. During the Civil War, the U.S. Army's chief of ordnance, General James Ripley, opposed repeating weapons like Colt's as a "great evil" that would waste ammunition; he preferred rifled flintlocks that a shooter could carefully and accurately aim. (For this, he was burnt in effigy three times from the Springfield Armory flagpole.) Prior to World War I, the army's chief of staff, Brigadier General J. Franklin Bell, noted that the army lacked a doctrine or even a plan for distribution of machine guns. And General Douglas MacArthur, prior to the Second World War, passed on the .276 Pedersen rifle in favor of the M1 Garand, which fired a larger bullet that flew flatter and farther.

This emphasis on accuracy wasn't without reason. The Minié ball, a groundbreaking conical bullet that loaded easier and flew more aerodynamically, was used with rifles during the Civil War and quickly proved the virtues of increasing range and accuracy by killing men by the tens of thousands. It made Napoleonic infantry tactics obsolete because infantry in the defense could fire upon rushing enemy troops, like those in the famously doomed Pickett's Charge, many times before the attackers reached the defensive line. Relatively few men died of bayonet wounds in the Civil War. They never got close enough, and the Minié ball is a major reason why.

But a narrow focus on accuracy obscured the increasingly critical role that would be played on the battlefield by weapons capable of providing a high *volume* of fire, even when that fire wasn't being directed at individual targets. As head-on assaults became suicidal, soldiers stopped firing at each other from close ranks and shifted to a dispersed line firing from behind covered positions, whether those consisted of walls, trees, rocks, and fences, or elaborate defensive fortifications. Instead of charging, tactics developed in which one group of soldiers would mass fires on an enemy position to keep their heads down and allow another unit to move forward safely. Studies showed that suppressive fire of this type was often done with the soldiers not even putting their weapons' sights to their eyes.

The other unit maneuvering into position under the cover of suppression was then meant to employ precision fire to kill the enemy, though this fire was far less precise than military trainers trumpeting slogans like "One shot, one kill" liked to think. Multiple studies of battles in World War II showed that most bullet hits were random, like shrapnel wounds, and happened at short range, though as Solly Zuckerman, the father of modern wound ballistics, drily noted, "Soldiers took more than a little convincing in those days that the rifle was not a precision weapon under battle conditions."

The combat veteran Brian Van Reet has described how, during the Iraq War, he and the men he served with "fired nearly blindly, under the influence of a strange and numbing feeling of terror, rage and exhilaration. Under these conditions, few of us really knew whom, if anyone, we had hit." Throughout the twentieth century, generals who purchased weapons they imagined would be fired by a series of individual soldiers carefully aiming at their individual enemies instead often found themselves commanding terrified groups of men surging with adrenaline, which increased their heart rates, redirected blood from their extremities, and impaired their fine motor control as they sprayed gunfire in the direction of their foes.

This disconnect between theory and practice led to a crisis early in the Vietnam War. American troops were armed with big, heavy, and extremely accurate M14 rifles. The Vietnamese had AK-47s, a sturdy, reliable weapon a child could (and often did) use. AK-47s were terribly inaccurate—during a military firing test in 1969, even expert shooters struggled to put ten consecutive rounds on target from three hundred meters—but the military quickly concluded that the M14 was, as then secretary of defense Robert McNamara put it, "definitely inferior in firepower and combat effectiveness" to the AK. The M14 had too much recoil to be fired effectively in automatic, and its heavy rounds imposed logistical limits on how much ammo could be carried. In fielding the M14, American soldiers had, as C. J. Chivers has written, fallen victim to the "romance" of "old-fashioned rifles and the sharp-shooting riflemen who carried them," when what they needed was an easy-to-handle assault rifle that could help give them fire superiority in close, terrifying encounters in dense jungles.

And so the military rushed into production the ArmaLite AR-15, later given the military designation M16, a semiautomatic, magazine-fed, gas-operated assault rifle. An accurate weapon with smaller rounds that could be carried in greater numbers than those of AKs, and which caused less recoil during firing, it was an elegantly de-signed machine. In theory, it would help win the war, if only Vietnam were the sort of war that could be won with a better rifle. In reality, the AR-15's triumph came not at war, but in peacetime America.

AR-15–STYLE WEAPONS ARE currently the most popular rifle in the United States. And when the Las Vegas shooter looked to arm himself with lightweight and versatile weapons suitable for inflicting mass death, he went with descendants of the ArmaLite AR-15.

On a civilian AR-15, a mechanical block requires the shooter to pull the trigger to release another bullet, thanks to the Firearm Owners' Protection Act of 1986, which banned the transfer or possession of machine guns. Clever gun enthusiasts figured out how to bypass this with a device known as a bump stock—which uses the energy of the rifle's recoil to assist in bumping the trigger against the shooter's finger—and which helped the Las Vegas shooter achieve something like fully automated rifle fire. The original military version of the AR-15, the M16, can fire eight hundred rounds per minute; an unmodified civilian AR-15 can fire forty-five to sixty per minute; and an AR-15 with a bump stock can fire somewhere between four hundred and eight hundred rounds per minute.

Because the device causes the rifle to slide forward and backward as the weapon fires, accuracy is diminished. In the aftermath of the shooting, this spurred some, like Georgia politician Michael Williams, to argue that the use of a bump stock "actually prevented more casualties . . . due to its inconsistency, inaccuracy, and lack of control."

This betrays a basic ignorance about guns. The bump stock effectively turns the AR-15 into a machine gun capable of "area fire," which is far different from the point target aiming and killing we are familiar with in action movies and television shows. In fact, one of the early innovations in automatic fire was to remove the human element in aiming altogether: Soldiers in the First World War traversed their target areas by applying a "two-inch tap" to the breeches of their machine guns, sending them two inches to the right or left. The gunner—who military historian John Keegan characterized as less of a soldier than a "machine-minder"—would tap repeatedly, until the gun reached a stop placed at its firing limit; then he would begin tapping in the opposite direction. In this way, the area in front of the gun could be blanketed with bullets without the gunner having eyes on any particular target. Since each round had a slightly different trajectory, the target zone would be saturated with fire, striking the ground in a pattern much like the blast of a shotgun. Managing this deadly area of impact, known as "the beaten zone," became crucial to the theory of machine-gun employment. As one Japanese officer put it during the Russo-Japanese War, the machine gun "can be made to sprinkle its shot as roads are watered with a hose."

This is how the Las Vegas shooter was using his weapon. As Lieutenant Colonel Arthur B. Alphin explained to the *Los Angeles Times*, "He was not aiming at any individual person. He was just throwing bullets in a huge 'beaten zone.'" And since it was a civilian target, with huge masses of people bunched together in ways soldiers had long ago learned to avoid, the accuracy of an individual round was immaterial. It was the rate of fire that mattered most.

By the end of the night, the shooter had killed 58 people and injured 422. There was nothing particularly remarkable about the shooter's skills; his lethality was primarily a function of the sheer number of rounds he could put downrange. Far from the expert long-range rifleman of Western lore, he was little more than the "machine-minder" of World War I, the human hand initiating a mechanical process designed to inflict death at an industrial scale.

II. SPIN AND YAW

There was something peculiar about the injured man—or, rather, something peculiar about how badly he was injured. Examining the X-rays, Solly Zuckerman saw only a small metal fragment, barely larger than a pinhead, lodged in the man's kidney. Other soldiers Zuckerman examined—men injured during the evacuation of Dunkirk, in

1940—had similar injuries. Usually, fragments from exploding shells and grenades were only considered dangerous if they weighed more than one twenty-fifth of an ounce, or 1133 milligrams. And yet, among those Zuckerman examined, he found a soldier who had been severely injured by a shard weighing less than 10 milligrams; another's forearm had been shattered by a minute metal splinter. According to the science of ballistics, such injuries made no sense.

At the time, Zuckerman worked as a scientist for the British government, devising experiments to help the war effort. The grisly and at times strange work meant examining countless cadavers and deliberately killing an inordinate number of small animals (who, given rationing, were often then eaten). Zuckerman, whose memoirs are written in the cool tone of a man who has long learned to see horrific violence as a scientific problem first and a tragedy a distant second, determined everything from how much explosive pressure was required to kill 50 percent of those directly exposed to a blast (500 pounds per square inch), to the percentage of bombs that could be successfully dropped on a target with a radial area of a thousand yards (80), to whether using a large pendulum hammer to instantaneously accelerate a monkey to 10.8 feet per second would cause ill effects (it did not). The goal was learning how much force living bodies could take, and where they were most vulnerable, information essential for both offensive campaigns and for the protection of civilians. His memoranda advised the Royal Air Force in maximizing casualties during bombing runs, and he helped design the iconic "Zuckerman helmet," a steel helmet worn by civilians and civil defense organizations designed to protect the head and neck area from falling debris and masonry during enemy raids.

But the ruinous fragments recovered from soldiers at Dunkirk would lead him to perform a set of experiments critical to the development of small-arms weapons. Along with Colonel Paul Libessart, a French engineer who fled to England after the fall of France, Zuckerman was on the cusp of transforming wound ballistics—the study of the manner in which projectiles damage human bodies.

Weapons researchers had long struggled to define and understand the lethality of projectiles. In the nineteenth century, the lethality of a weapon was often judged by how deep its bullets penetrated into wood; in the 1880s, the metric shifted to whether a bullet could kill a cavalry horse—this was said to capture a bullet's "stopping power." Although the concept of stopping power was vague, it was clear that some bullets and weapons had more of it than others. "There can be little doubt that from a humanitarian point of view the Lee-Metford rifle is a perfect weapon," Surgeon-Lieutenant Jay Gould noted, in 1895, after examining tribesmen injured during the British Chitral Expedition in northern India; the bullets it fired often passed cleanly through bodies and bone rather than sending bone fragments in all directions. To Gould, this tendency was disconcerting: "Would it stop a rush?" he asked.

Soldiers tended to assume that stopping a rush required heavier, more powerful bullets. In the first half of the twentieth century, American researchers conducted experiments of dubious value designed to prove this point. They hung cadavers in the air and shot them while observers estimated how far the corpses swung; they shot cows and observed the effects (universally bad for the cows). Eventually, the U.S. Army declared kinetic energy the crucial factor in bullet lethality. After a series of experiments, they concluded that fifty-eight foot-pounds of kinetic energy were enough to ensure death. (A foot-pound represents the oomph required to raise one pound a distance of one foot.)

The Dunkirk injuries convinced Zuckerman that something was missing from this story. The overall kinetic energy of a bullet (which can be determined with a simple equation involving the bullet's mass and velocity) might be less important than how much of that bullet's energy was transferred while inside the body.

Zuckerman's initial experiments were improvisational but effective: He and his team would fire a steel ball into a phone book, then repeat the shot with the book placed behind a block of gelatin, which represented the body. They'd count how many pages the ball had penetrated in both cases, using the difference in page count as a proxy for deceleration. That allowed them to determine how much kinetic energy had been transferred to the gelatin. Zuckerman's suspicion was that this was the critical factor in wounding.

Later experiments showed this in greater detail. Zuckerman shot small metal balls through the limbs of unfortunate rabbits. By means of a technique called shadowgraphy—the analysis of shadows cast by bodies in rapid motion—Zuckerman showed that in the split seconds after impact, the limbs "ballooned due to the formation of an internal cavity."

Wounds caused by firearms had long been identified with the "permanent cavity" created by a bullet—that is, with the tissue that was crushed by the bullet itself. Zuckerman's images captured a different kind of injury: a "temporary cavity," formed when the slowing bullet transferred energy to the surrounding soft tissue. Just as a diver entering a pool imparts her momentum to the water, creating ripples, so a bullet imparts momentum to particles of blood, spleen, brain, and so on that surround its entry point. The ripples produce blunt trauma, pulping tissue and breaking bones. That's why tiny slivers of metal could shatter a man's arm. Stopping power wasn't just about how powerful your bullet was, but about how much it stopped inside the human body.

A DECADE LATER, Eugene Stoner, a Marine Corps veteran of the Pacific Theater in World War II, was tinkering in his garage. A shy, reserved, yet opinionated man, Stoner lacked formal engineering education. He'd worked his way up through a machine shop building prototypes at the Fairchild Engine and Airplane Corporation and, despite the objections of coworkers over his lack of an engineering degree, into their engineering department.

That experience with aircraft, as well as his more general lack of concern with standard ways of doing things, led him to a series of innovations in an unrelated industry—firearms. Using advanced alloys and lightweight parts common in aeronautics but new to rifles, he developed a firing mechanism for a lightweight rifle that would, years later, become the dominant firearm in both the American military and American society writ large.

Success was slow in coming. Stoner's first prototype burst a barrel in army tests, and the weight of U.S. military opinion was in favor of the heavier, more powerful M14. But a small insurgency within the military was pushing a novel idea known as SCHV—or small caliber, high velocity. One of the officers in favor of the idea, General Willard G. Wyman, met with Stoner and asked him to modify his weapon for a redesigned .222 Remington round weighing only one tenth of an ounce—less than half the weight of the Viet Cong's bullet of choice.

Stoner's modified rifle, the now-famous AR-15, would fire its 5.56-millimeter round at over 3,200 feet per second—nearly three times the speed of sound—giving it comparable overall kinetic energy to the slower AK round, and perhaps even greater wounding capabilities.

As Stoner would later explain to Congress, smaller bullets have distinct advantages. "Bullets are stabilized to fly through the air, and not through water, or a body," he explained. "When they hit something, they immediately go unstable. . . . A little bullet, being as it has a low mass, it senses an instability situation faster and reacts much faster."

Picture yourself in a theater when a gunman bursts in and begins firing into the audience. A round strikes your side, traveling in a straight path through flesh, muscle, and intestine for 20 centimeters before exiting your body. If that bullet is the longer, heavier AK bullet, which only begins tumbling at depths of greater than 20 centimeters, it will travel through your body relatively hydrodynamically, its point mostly forward, like a professional diver entering a pool with little splash. If that bullet is from an AR-15, however, the bullet will begin tumbling at around 11 centimeters, like an out-of-control race car spinning as it moves forward along the track. By around 18 centimeters, the bullet will be at full yaw, tilted 180 degrees, doing a belly flop into the pool of fluids inside your body. Here, the bullet is transferring the maximum energy to your inner organs, creating shock waves of pressure strong enough to sever muscle tissue or break apart your spleen. If a second bullet strikes your head, the pressure can shatter your skull or, short of that, squeeze brain tissue out through your sinuses. Adding to the injuries, the bullet often fragments inside the human body, scattering small pieces of metal outward and further increasing the damage.

Colt, which had suffered a million-dollar loss in 1963 and had bought the rights to the AR-15 in a gamble, went on a unique marketing campaign. They won a convert in the higher ranks of the Air Force by inviting General Curtis LeMay to a Fourth of July shooting party, where the general fired the AR-15 into watermelons, creating bright red, juicy explosions with each successful shot. The rifle was then submitted to military tests in which processed human heads from India, "unbleached and undefatted," were encased in ballistic gelatin and shot with rifle rounds at various distances. This and other tests convinced the military they had a solution to the small-arms imbalance in Vietnam, and the AR-15 was hastily adapted into the military's weapon of choice, the M16. The rifle was fielded, tragically, before even the normal debugging of weapons malfunctions had been done, which led to the weapon breaking down in the field, jamming, or refusing to fire in the middle of firefights. "You know what killed most of us?" said one survivor of a hill fight in Vietnam in 1967 that left over one hundred and fifty Marines dead. "Our own rifle."

Colt, meanwhile, would post $12 million in profit in 1967, nearly doubling its profits from the year before. Stoner would go from his garage tinkering to a life of celebrity, wealth, and a private plane he enjoyed piloting himself. And though service members continued to distrust the weapon that had failed them so badly, the kinks would eventually get worked out. The American military still uses a variant of Stoner's weapon, firing smaller yet extremely deadly rounds.

In a landmark 1962 study of wound ballistics, Lieutenant General Leonard Heaton, the surgeon general of the U.S. Army, surveyed these kinds of wounds. "The message which this volume contains for the physician who will be treating the wounds of war is clear," he wrote. "War wounds, in many respects, are different from those found in peacetime civilian practice."

In Heaton's day, of course, hardly any civilians had firearms capable of producing such effects. The situation is different now, and not simply because of the rapid profusion of AR-style weapons, 15 to 20 million of which are in circulation in the United States. In Las Vegas, the gunman's firearm, with its high rate of fire, made him more lethal. So did the design of the more than 1,100 rounds of ammunition he fired upon the crowd. The bullets flew from his hotel room with their noses pointed forward, spinning and traveling several times the speed of sound. Upon striking flesh, they began to yaw, smashing through bone, slowing as they rotated, imparting energy to the surrounding tissue and shredding organs. Of the 104 shooting victims seen at the UMC Trauma Center in Las Vegas that night, more than 30 had critical injuries, and over a dozen needed operations from orthopedists or cardiovascular or abdominal surgeons. Chest tubes had to be inserted to drain internal bleeding; bowels had to be carefully resected by doctors working with needle and thread. The injuries were just as horrific as intended; they were a matter of design.

III. DISPERSAL

For Samuel Colt, the decade of the 1840s began poorly and violently. In 1841, his brother John murdered a man, and not even with a firearm, but with a hatchet. John salted the hacked-up corpse, packed it in a case, and shipped it to New Orleans, only to be caught, tried, and sentenced to death. The year 1842 brought two more disasters. The day of his brother's scheduled execution, a fire broke out at the prison, and after it was controlled, John Colt's corpse was found in his cell with a knife in his heart. Then there was the end of the Seminole War. Colt had supplied repeating rifles for the campaign hunting Seminoles throughout the Everglades, and the guns performed a little too well. "The thing was so good that it ruined itself," Colt's lawyer, Edward Dickerson, admitted. As Colt later put it, "By exterminating the Indians, and bringing the war rapidly to an end, the market for the arms was destroyed."

Colt's problem wasn't about technical engineering or industrial process. His weapons had proved themselves in multiple conflicts, could be produced at a reasonable cost, and yet could not find a mass market because no such market existed. Historically, the U.S. appetite for guns had been so anemic it had been considered a security liability. In 1756, a report on the military preparedness of the colonies found that, out of thirty-six thousand militia members, "not above half that number" were armed. Those who were often had broken, ungainly, outdated, badly designed, or poorly maintained weapons. The frontier was even less well armed. In 1776, the governor of Rhode Island told George Washington that colonists out west thought themselves in such "a perfect state of security" that they had "disposed of their arms so generally" as to render them effectively "disarmed." Washington himself complained of the scarcity of gunsmiths and guns; and the colonies ultimately had to rely on France for the purchase of tens of thousands of muskets. Simply put, early America had no gun culture. But Colt was an inventor. He could invent one.

The first step was expanding beyond the narrow hunt for U.S. government contracts. "The Government may go to the Devil and I will go my own way," he had once vowed. Now he made steps to make it a reality. First he put the business on a firmer financial footing by selling abroad. In the mid-1800s, he supplied guns to soldiers of fortune in Cuba, to the British in South Africa, to "men of brains" in Mexico, and smuggled guns into Russia in bales of cotton.

Then he built up the U.S. civilian market. Here, his background as a traveling performer came in handy. Before he'd ever started selling guns, Colt had traveled America as "Dr. Coult of London, New York, and Calcutta," administering nitrous oxide to spectators. The gas, he promised, would help them laugh, dance, sing, and perform startling feats of "muscular exertion." At one point, he was pressed into service to cure riverboat patients with suspected yellow fever (he administered laughing gas—not a known cure). The experience had taught him about advertising, about the flair sometimes necessary to stoke the public's fancy, and about shamelessness.

He pioneered the use of celebrity endorsements to sell his products, commissioning the well-known painter George Catlin to paint self-portraits in which Catlin shot buffalo, deer, and jaguars with Colt revolvers. Colt had himself named a lieutenant colonel (by the state of Connecticut) and used the honorific to introduce himself at foreign courts, presenting European royalty with lavishly engraved Colts. When a local clergyman's home was burglarized, Colt sent over a revolver along with a message declaring the gun "my latest work on 'Moral Reform.'" It wasn't the first time Colt had seized upon a well-known crime as part of a marketing ploy. During his brother's trial for a murder in which no firearms were involved, Colt took the opportunity to demonstrate his weapons in the courtroom.

He also designed his own advertisements, coining the phrase "new and improved" to entice buyers, and hired writers to pen magazine pieces about his guns. To amp sales, he was happy to suggest dangers around every corner; at one point he wrote to Mormon leader Brigham Young, advising him to buy Colt revolvers as a defense against "raids of savages" and "white marauders." Later he would name several streets of Coltsville, his factory town, after Native American warriors—Sequassen, Wawarme, Masseek, and Curcombe—a tribute to the extent to which images of Indian fighting had burnished his weapon's reputation.

"What Colt invented," the historian William Hosley wrote, "was a system of myths, symbols, stagecraft, and distribution" promising that ownership of a Colt would provide "access to the celebrity, glamour and dreams of its namesake." And other gun manufacturers soon picked up on the increasingly prevalent promise of Colt's advertising:

that his weapons could preserve individual agency in a hostile world. Winchester, who was also trying to grow the civilian market by adopting a policy of "scattering our guns"—deliberately rejecting high volume orders in favor of smaller buyers who might disperse the weaponry more broadly—started advertising his guns as ideal for a "single individual, traveling through a wild country." Gun manufacturers more broadly began to employ "predicament" advertising, in which lone travelers face bears, outlaws, or "savages," and the only path out is through violence. And after Colt's death in 1862, Colt's Patent Fire-Arms Manufacturing Company employed marketing that deliberately blended the military and civilian domains. The Winchester Repeating Arms Company advertised its weapons "for military and sporting purposes," but the famous Colt Single Action Army model, dubbed "the Peacemaker," took the idea a step further when it was marketed as a weapon "for all who travel among dangerous communities."

The American ideals of freedom and equality were recast, by gunmakers, in martial terms; self-reliance, respect, and freedom of movement were tied to the capacity to kill. "Abe Lincoln may have freed all men," one advertisement read, "but Sam Colt made them equal." By the late nineteenth century, the mythology of the hyperviolent West was so embedded in American consciousness that Teddy Roosevelt would construct a notion of American identity around it. "White men and red fought one another whenever they met," he would write, arguing that the heat of this continual battle on the frontier "weld[ed] together into one people the representatives of these numerous and widely different races." Americanness, and American principles like equality, were repackaged as a product of violence.

In reality, Indian tribes like the Comanches were decimated less by firearms than by disease. Still, gun companies wrote themselves into history: in ads, dime-store novels, and movies. The Winchester

Model 1873 Repeating Rifle, part of a deliberate campaign in which specially promoted guns found their way into the hands of celebrities like Billy the Kid and Buffalo Bill, was mythologized as "The Gun That Won the West." On the strength of this myth, Winchester sold almost thirty times as many guns in 1914 as it had in 1875. And after World War I, the Thompson Machine Gun, developed as a trench-clearing tool, went to market with advertisements showing cowboys defending their ranches against marauders and text proclaiming it "the ideal weapon for the protection of large estates, ranches, plantations, etc."

No wonder, then, that in 1968 a spokesman from the National Rifle Association would tell Congress that American gun culture was the result of a "very special relationship between a man and his gun—atavistic, with its roots deep in history." The roots may have been more in pop culture than in the effectively "disarmed" frontier of 1776, but those roots did go back over a century.

By the crime wave of the late 1980s and early '90s, then, the image of the frontier hero, fending off nonwhite marauders with firepower that enabled him to "travel among dangerous communities," was ready for repurposing by an industry facing a decline in hunting sales. The NRA ran ads asking, "Why can't a policeman be there when you need him?" and "Should you shoot a rapist before he cuts your throat?" And then, after a rising wave of antigovernment feeling sparked by the 1993 shootout between members of David Koresh's cult, the Branch Davidians, and agents of the Bureau of Alcohol, Tobacco and Firearms, the NRA ran ads asking, "What's the first step to a police state?" Guns were no longer tools for frontier spaces government hadn't reached; they were a necessity for all spaces at all times. When crime and authoritarianism run rampant, the Wild West is everywhere.

Unfortunately for gun manufacturers, crime fell, and with it gun sales, going from just over 5 million in 1994 to a low point of under 3 million in 2001. Of course, the terrorist attacks of late 2001 brought more reasons to be afraid, and gun sales began modestly climbing again. But it was only in 2008 that the gun industry began undergoing a truly seismic transformation, something that would excite the American demand for guns like nothing before. Within the industry, they called it the "Barack Boom."

The election of America's first black president coincided with what one gun industry newsletter referred to as an "incessant consumer demand for high-capacity pistols and military-style rifles." During the 2008 campaign, the NRA warned that never in its history had it "faced a presidential candidate—and hundreds of candidates running for other offices—with such a deep-rooted hatred of firearm freedoms." In 2013, despite decades-low crime rates, the head of the NRA claimed that, under Obama, "Latin American drug gangs have invaded every city of significant size in the United States." In 2014, the NRA put out a special issue of its magazine featuring an ISIS fighter on the cover, and the proclamation: "A Dangerous World Is Closing In." Marketing and political messaging merged. When Springfield launched an ad campaign trumpeting its legacy of making firearms "for the independent and the free," a January 2017 issue of Shooting Industry approvingly quoted commenters on the campaign who suggested it might help people "realize they shouldn't rely on the government for protection." As another commenter argued, "If we don't get younger people into self defense and shooting sports, we'll be overwhelmingly outnumbered on election day."

Meanwhile, advertising cast guns as a route to self-sufficiency, freedom, and manliness; as tools for protection from crime and resistance against a possibly tyrannical government; and as equipment used by active-duty military who worked for that possibly tyrannical government. Thus, in 2010, an ad for Bushmaster could declare that, with ownership of its assault rifle, you can "consider your man card reissued"; in 2012, Sig Sauer could superimpose its handgun over an image of a fighter pilot ("His other weapon is an F/A 18"); and Remington could tell politicians, over an image of a scoped rifle, "Attention Politicians. Over 5,000,000 Sold. The World's Largest Army Ain't in China." By the last year of Obama's second term in office, gun manufacturers would produce a record 11,497,441 guns for domestic consumption.

The end result is a massive, culturally immovable, civilian American firearms market, with a heavy emphasis on the military-grade equipment that the Las Vegas shooter used to commit mass murder. American civilians now hold 46 percent of the world's total civilian firearms; those firearms are orders of magnitude more deadly than anything conceivable before the mid-nineteenth century. And this market has been created out of a mixture of myths about American history, antigovernment rhetoric, paranoia, fear of crime, fascination with military hardware, and appeals to the insecurities of American men. These myths are the software American consumers are buying along with their hardware.

WHEN JOHN BILLINGTON came upon John Newcomen, he was only armed because he was out hunting deer. His weapon did not promise him his manhood, or protection from his fellow colonists, or protection from the coercive state under which he suffered; it did not claim to be the bedrock of his freedom or the means by which all men would be made to treat him as an equal. When Billington pulled its trigger, the bullet he sent forth was a simple metal sphere traveling less than half the speed of the bullets fired in the Las Vegas shooting. Unlike those rounds, it moved awkwardly through the air. In the body, it damaged only what was directly in its path. And it was a lone projectile. It would have taken Billington six hours to fire as many bullets as the Las Vegas gunman had. Billington might have had a tool suitable for murder—but not mass murder.

The tools today's Americans buy and sell by the millions are perfectly suitable for mass murder, and their very ubiquity is harnessed as a reason for selling more of them. "The only way to stop a bad guy with a gun is with a good guy with a gun," we are told. (With modern firearms, of course, it's not too hard for a bad guy to squeeze off hundreds of rounds before a good guy can intervene.) This state of affairs is good for the continued development and sale of weaponry. Samuel Colt's market was easy to saturate because his guns killed their targets too quickly. The civilian market he helped create is bottomless. Untethered to war, it finds its own targets. Who knows what further innovations the future may bring?

III | WRITING

AFTER WAR, A FAILURE OF THE IMAGINATION

FEBRUARY 8, 2014

I could never imagine what you've been through," she said.

As a former Marine who served in Iraq, I'd heard the sentiment before—it's the civilian counterpart to the veteran's "You wouldn't know, you weren't there." But this time it struck an especially discordant note. This woman was a friend. She'd read something I'd written about Iraq—about the shocked numbness I'd felt looking at the victims of a suicide bombing—and it had resonated. As a survivor of child abuse, she knew feelings of shocked numbness far better than I did. And yet, midway through recounting some of what happened to her as a young girl, she said it again: "I'm sorry. I don't mean to compare my experience to yours. I could never imagine what you've been through."

It felt inappropriate to respond, "Sure you could." I'd had a mild deployment. She'd mainly have to imagine long hours at a cheap plywood desk in a cheap plywood hut in the middle of a desert. True, there were a handful of alarming but anticlimactic mortar attacks on my forward operating base, and the wounded and damaged bodies I saw at the trauma center, but that was all. Her childhood, though, was full of experiences I couldn't have handled as an adult, let alone as a child. And what was particularly bewildering was that, even as my friend was insisting that what I'd been through was beyond the limits of imagination, she never once told me, "You aren't a victim of child abuse. You couldn't understand." She wanted me to understand. At the very least, she wanted me to try.

I know an airman who suffered a traumatic brain injury during training just a few years after being in a car accident where he watched his twin brother die. When he tells people about the TBI and the accident and his service, he invariably gets the "I could never imagine" line. "It makes me angry," he told me. Sure, he wants to say, you don't think you could understand, but what if I want you to?

It's a difficult spot to be in, for both. The civilian wants to respect what the veteran has gone through. The veteran wants to protect memories that are painful and sacred to him from outside judgment. But the result is the same: the veteran in a corner by himself, able to proclaim about war but not discuss it, and the civilian shut out from a conversation about one of the most morally fraught activities our nation engages in—war.

The notion that war forever separates veterans from the rest of mankind has long been embedded in our collective consciousness. After World War I, the poet and veteran Siegfried Sassoon wrote, "The man who really endured the war at its worst was everlastingly differentiated from everyone except his fellow soldiers." During World War II, Hemingway called combat "that thing which no one knows about who has not done it." After Vietnam, Tim O'Brien claimed that a true war story can't even be told, because "sometimes it's just beyond telling." Given the way American history, unlike Iraqi or Afghan history, allows for a neat division between soldiers who see war and civilians who don't, it's not surprising that the idea has taken root.

When I returned from Iraq, people often asked me what it was like, usually followed by, "How are we doing over there?" And I'd tell them. I'd explain in bold, confident terms about the surge and the Sunni Awakening. The Iraq I returned from was, in my mind, a fairly simple place. By which I mean it had little relationship to reality. It's only with time and the help of smart, empathetic friends willing to pull through many serious conversations that I've been able to learn more about what I witnessed. And many of those conversations were with friends who'd never served.

We pay political consequences when civilians are excused or excluded from discussion of war. After all, veterans are no more or less trustworthy than any other group of fallible human beings. Southern veterans of the Civil War claimed the Confederacy was a noble lost cause. Nazi leaders who had served in World War I claimed that the German troops had all but won the war, only to be stabbed in the back by civilians in thrall to Jewish interests. The notion that the veteran is an unassailable authority on the experience of war shuts down conversation. But in a democracy, no one, not even a veteran, should have the last word.

The problem is compounded on a personal level. If we fetishize trauma as incommunicable, then survivors are trapped—unable to feel truly known by their nonmilitary friends and family. At a recent Veterans Day performance put on by Arts in the Armed Forces, Adam Driver, the organization's founder, a former Marine turned actor, spoke of his feelings of alienation after leaving the Corps. "Not being able to express the anger, confusion and loneliness I felt was challenging," he said, until theater exposed him "to playwrights and characters and plays that had nothing to do with the military, that were articulating experiences I had in the military, that before to me were indescribable."

It's a powerful moment when you discover a vocabulary exists for something you'd thought incommunicably unique. Personally, I felt it reading Joseph Conrad's *Lord Jim*. I have friends who've found themselves described in everything from science fiction to detective novels. This self-recognition through others is not simply a by-product of art—it's the whole point. Hegel once wrote, "The nature of humanity is to drive men to agreement with one another, and humanity's existence lies only in the commonality of consciousness that has been brought about."

To enter into that commonality of consciousness, though, veterans need an audience that is both receptive and critical. Believing war is beyond words is an abrogation of responsibility—it lets civilians off the hook from trying to understand, and veterans off the hook from needing to explain. You don't honor someone by telling them, "I can never imagine what you've been through." Instead, listen to their story and try to imagine being in it, no matter how hard or uncomfortable that feels. If the past ten years have taught us anything, it's that in the age of an all-volunteer military, it is far too easy for Americans to send soldiers on deployment after deployment without making a serious effort to imagine what that means. We can do better.

FACT AND FICTION

OCTOBER 10, 2015

Sometimes in interviews I catch myself speaking of my book of short stories about the Iraq War as though it is a kind of literary journalism. I want people to think about their recent history, imagine the lives of soldiers, and get a sense of what it's like to go to war. And I do want those things, since having a richer sense of war experience is essential to having a richer understanding our obligations toward a world wracked by war and political violence. But I'm always troubled by readings of war literature that begin and end with empathetic engagement. There's capturing authentic experience, and then there's doing the work of writing and reading fiction. "What it's like" is a means, after all, and often it's a slippery one.

In Wilfred Owen, what it's like is to be "Bent double, like old beggars under sacks, / Knock-kneed, coughing like hags . . . All went lame; all blind; / Drunk with fatigue; deaf even to the hoots / Of disappointed shells that dropped behind." And his poem, directed "to a certain Poetess" (the patriotic civilian poet Jessie Pope), tells the reader that if they too could "pace / Behind the wagon" or "watch the white eyes writhing in his face" or "hear, at every jolt, the blood / Come gargling from the froth-corrupted lungs," then they would not tell children "The old Lie: *Dulce et decorum est / Pro patria mori.*"

But for Ernst Jünger, here is what it was like to fight in the very same war: "The exchange of hand grenades reminded me of fencing with foils; you needed to jump and stretch, almost as in a ballet. . . . In those moments, I was capable of seeing the dead—I jumped over them with every stride—without horror. They lay there in the relaxed and softly spilled attitude that characterizes those moments in which life takes its leave."

And for Ford Madox Ford, also a veteran of the First World War, "what's it's like" was to hang about:

> The process of the eternal waiting that is War. You hung about and you hung about, and you kicked your heels and you kicked your heels: waiting for Mills bombs to come, or for jam, or for generals, or for the tanks, or transport, or the clearance of the road ahead. You waited in offices under the eyes of somnolent orderlies, under fire on the banks of canals, you waited in hotels, dug-outs, tin sheds, ruined houses. There will be no man who survives of His Majesty's Armed Forces that shall not remember those eternal hours when Time itself stayed still as the true image of bloody War!

The sheer variety of experience in war is enough to make a modern war writer throw up their hands. "War is hell," wrote Tim O'Brien, "but that's not the half of it, because war is mystery and terror and

adventure and courage and discovery and holiness and pity and despair and longing and love. War is nasty; war is fun. War is thrilling;
war is drudgery. War makes you a man; war makes you dead." I've
spent countless hours trying to evoke, with as much focus as possible,
the exact sensations of any variety of given moments of war. And even
if when I finish I feel I've succeeded, I often then go and throw those
pages out, because what good are mere sensations?

In a 2010 essay for *The Guardian*, the writer Geoff Dyer argued that
the great war literature of modern times didn't come to us through
fiction or poetry, but through journalism. He writes, "If there were
ever a time when the human stories contained within historical
events—what Packer calls 'the human heart of the matter'—could
only be assimilated and comprehended when they had been processed
by a novel (*War and Peace* is the supreme example), that time has
passed." For Iraq, he points readers toward Dexter Filkins's *The Forever
War* and David Finkel's *The Good Soldiers*. For Vietnam, he holds up
Michael Herr's classic *Dispatches* over the work of Tim O'Brien, Robert Stone, and Jayne Anne Phillips.

On the other side of the debate, you have Robert Graves arguing
that "the memoirs of a man who went through some of the worst experiences of trench warfare are not truthful if they do not contain a
high proportion of falsities," and Tim O'Brien, in "How to Tell a True
War Story," declaring: "Happeningness is irrelevant. A thing may
happen and be a total lie; another thing may not happen and be truer
than the truth."

Personally I don't recognize a stark distinction between the
various sorts of war literature. I love Finkel's *The Good Soldiers* for precisely the same reason I love Céline's *Journey to the End of the Night*—
both books leave me profoundly unsettled about issues of war and
peace that I'd previously taken for granted. The attempt to reproduce,

with as exacting a verisimilitude as possible, what it's like to serve in war is only valuable to me if it guides the reader toward the kind of collision of values and the destruction of ideologies that war experience sometimes brings about. If we do nothing with the knowledge other than manifest a sort of weak empathy, if the reader is not unsettled at a more fundamental level than mere discomfort at the effective description of violence, then the writer has done the reader little service.

I don't read Shūsaku Endō's *Silence* out of a deep need to understand the experience of seventeenth-century Japanese Christians any more than I read George Eliot's *Middlemarch* out of a burning desire to understand ninteenth-century provincial English politics. Why should it function any differently for war writers? Even for writers dealing with events in recent memory, it's difficult to plan for how your work may factor into political understandings of policy. World War II veteran Joseph Heller, for example, could hardly have predicted the ways in which his 1961 novel *Catch-22* would get taken up by antiwar segments of the Vietnam generation. And it is worth noting that Heller once claimed that "the antiwar and antigovernment feelings in the book belong to the period following World War II: the Korean War, the cold war, and the fifties." So (if we choose to believe him) he didn't even mean for his World War II novel to tell us much about World War II. And yet, precisely for this reason, *Catch-22* ended up reading like a dispatch from the future.

Where, then, do the facts come in? In the writing I do, research factors heavily. I'm looking for real-life situations that might offer fruitful avenues for exploring questions about war, about masculinity, about violence. When I learned that one of the tactics during the Battle of Fallujah was to have psychological operations specialists shout insults over loudspeakers, that offered me one tool for thinking about the act of killing. When I talked to an artilleryman about being part of a team firing an incredibly deadly weapon toward a target he'd never see that was miles away, that offered me another tool. The accumulation of these tools does not make a story, but it is a start. And in addition to looking for these situations, I obsess over small details, because small details can carry tremendous emotional weight. To Vietnam veterans who received the first trial run of M16s, the difference between the M16 and the M14 was not a numeral, but life and death, the difference between a reliable weapon and an unreliable one. If you fudge those details, you can lose your reader's trust.

So there are plenty of facts in my fiction. A small part of my writing is wrenched out of my experience, which I skeptically allow a certain bit of authority. Part of it comes from interviews with veterans, from books and articles I've read, from documentaries I've watched, and through half-remembered bits of late-night conversations in bars. What I'm looking for, though, is not enough information to allow me to create a near-documentary recounting of reality, but enough information to allow me to evade being totally captured by fact. I want enough knowledge about my subject that I feel confident making things up. If I know five compelling stories or details about, say, being a chaplain in the military, then I'll write a story in which I go in a straight line hitting those five points, and the character will feel lifeless. I need to get enough comfort with the world in order to ignore the things I know when the character starts to suggest other directions for me. And it's only when these departures happen that work starts to feel truly honest.

When we read Homer, we are reading the work of a poet who had no idea how the Trojan War was fought. He didn't know how chariots were used then, or what armor was worn, or that the Greeks of that age didn't fight in phalanxes. And yet every generation of warriors seems to rediscover the *Iliad* and find their own wars described within it. In my work I'm trying, through facts and through invention, to find some small piece of what Homer found in myth. It's a truth that often lies somewhere in between the facts, but doesn't necessarily rely on them.

PUBLIC RAGE WON'T SOLVE
ANY OF OUR PROBLEMS

OCTOBER 25, 2018

R ecently a friend asked me, with what I thought was a hint of suspicion in his voice, why my writing was so "apolitical." It's not the first time it's happened, but it always surprises me. I've written about military policy under both President Obama and President Trump. I've questioned what we're doing and tried to write about what flawed policy looks and feels like to those tasked with carrying it out. To me, this is inescapably and obviously engaged political speech.

But to my friend, a smart guy who nevertheless spends a surprising amount of his time online coming up with inventive ways to crassly insult his political enemies, there was something lacking. Something to do with my inclination to be "unfailingly polite," as he called it. I try to avoid making personal attacks, or casting my arguments in the typical good-evil binary of partisan politics. My friend is a veteran of a tough deployment to Afghanistan. He's acutely conscious of how thin our public discussion of the wars has been. And, more than anything, he's acutely conscious of the ways our collective failure as a society to demand serious oversight of the wars has direct, physical, violent impact on people we know and care about.

If you look back on the human waste of the past seventeen years and are not filled with rage, is there not something wrong with you? And if you want to be honest in public debate, if you don't want to engage in the kind of lies and obfuscations and doublespeak proliferating across our body politic, don't you have to let that rage slip into your speech?

It's a fair point. Rage seems like a perfectly natural and justified response to our broader political dysfunction. From health care to tax policy to climate change, we are failing to meaningfully address issues whose impact can be measured in human lives. And invitations to civil debate can sometimes be nothing more than a con carried out by malign actors within the system. The conservative entertainer Ann Coulter used to play a game where she'd say something horrible, and then, when questioned about it, shift to a thinly connected but defensible argument, like when she claimed on the *Today* show that she'd written that a group of politically active 9/11 widows were "enjoying their husbands' deaths" only to call attention to how they were "using their grief in order to make a political point." The game, one suspects, is less about sparking debate than indulging in a kind of performative contempt. So why play that game, when the simple extension of a middle finger is both easier and more honest? It will, at the very least, be more fun.

But performative rage is fun for both sides. A few months ago, I did a reading in Brooklyn with an author who'd written a harrowing indictment of our border policy. But because the author was once a Border Patrol agent, a group of young people showed up to protest.

Rather than a thoughtful discussion in which an insider explained how the U.S. brings its power to bear on the vulnerable, the audience sat through an often comic display of self-righteous slogan chanting. At one point, an audience member began cursing the protesters out in Spanish, ending his rant with, "Are white people always like this?" I could feel the audience's politics ticking slightly rightward. I doubt any immigrants were helped by the spectacle.

That kind of engagement in the public sphere takes the hard pragmatic choices of governance, in which we must make decisions about a set of complex issues for which we have imperfect information and no perfect solutions, and substitutes one simple question: Is my political adversary repellent? Or, even more to the point: Am I better than them? And the answer we want to give ourselves to that question is almost always yes.

RAGE IS A dangerous emotion, not simply because it can be destructive, but because it can be so easily satisfied with cheap targets. Like my friend who picks fights online, I'm a veteran. I know people who have been injured or killed overseas. I've seen the damage bombs wreak on the bodies of innocent civilians. And, yes, it fills me with rage. But if that rage is to mean anything, it means I cannot distract myself with the illusion of adjudicating past wrongs with artfully phrased put-downs. In a world where we are still at war, the most important question is, What do we do now? There the moral certainty of my rage must be met with humility about the limits of my knowledge.

I'll never forget the journalist Nir Rosen, who'd become something of a darling of the antiwar left for his well-informed criticisms of U.S. Middle East policy, delivering a blistering attack in front of the

Senate Committee on Foreign Relations two months after I returned from Iraq. Everything we had done during the thirteen months I'd spent overseas, it seemed, was morally corrupt, counterproductive, and dangerous. But when then-Senator Joe Biden put the ball in Rosen's court by asking, "Based on what you've said, there's really no hope, we should just get the hell out of there right now, right?" Rosen was stumped. He admitted that he didn't actually know what should be done, that withdrawal might lead to a spike in sectarian violence and that "it could be Rwanda the day the Americans leave." As a knowledgeable observer of a complex war, Rosen knew enough, despite his first impulse, to know he didn't have the answers.

Civility is a style of argument that implicitly welcomes response. It is a display of respect and tolerance, which make clear that you are engaging in a conversation, not delivering a last word. Unlike contempt, which generally seems less about your targets than about creating an ugly spectacle for your own partisans to enjoy, a civil argument is a plea to all fellow citizens to respond, even if in opposition. It invites the broader body of concerned citizens to fill in the gaps in my knowledge, to correct the flaws in my argument, and to continue to deliberate in a rapidly changing world.

Anytime we as a nation act in the world, we are met with a host of second- and third-order consequences, sometimes consequences of greater significance than what we initially set out to fix. The invasion of Iraq, and the rise of jihadism that followed, taught us that. Debates about how to respond to Saddam Hussein had to be followed by debates about the insurgency, the breakdown of governance, the value of international aid versus military action, the rising influence of Iran, the costs of inaction in Syria, and the escalating refugee crisis. Critics of today's policy may have useful information for tomorrow's problems.

Which means we should engage them in a style of discourse that isn't about "destroying" them but about inviting them to respond.

Whether this leads to electoral victories is another question altogether. The civil debates where good-faith participants collectively grope toward better answers to our most pressing challenges are happening in small corners of the public square. Meanwhile, we have a president who came to office flinging insults. Clearly, stoking rage and contempt in the public square can work. It excites us. It gives us courage to act in the face of uncertainty. We never fully know others, or their motivations, or the extent of their virtues and vices. But if instead of acknowledging that we reduce them to the least charitable caricature possible, it allows us to feel we're on certain ground. But we're never on certain ground. And while abandoning a process of thoughtful deliberation can win you power, what it can never do is give you a hope of using that power wisely.

VISIONS OF WAR AND PEACE: LITERATURE AND AUTHORITY IN WORLD WAR I

JUNE 30, 2019

I n the familiar literature, World War I comes to us, overwhelmingly, as muck and madness, an orgy of pointless violence, insanity on a civilizational scale as waves of young men were sent off with fine words into a meat grinder. It is blood gargling from "froth-corrupted lungs, obscene as cancer." It is the old battalion, "hanging on the old barbed wire." It is "strange hells within the minds war made," while an oblivious public back home remains smugly, and wrongly, certain that "chivalry redeems the wars."

In *Company K*, a brilliant and sadly underread novel by William March, who served in World War I with the Marines and was decorated with the Croix de Guerre, the Distinguished Service Cross, and the Navy Cross, a soldier tries a hand at writing an honest condolence letter after the death of a comrade. He writes:

> He died in agony, slowly. You'd never believe that he could live three hours, but he did. He lived three full hours

screaming and cursing by turns. He had nothing to hold on to, you see: He had learned long ago that what he had been taught to believe by you, his mother, who loved him, under the meaningless names of honor, courage and patriotism, were all lies . . .

This, according to much of the literature of World War I, is the bitter truth that the war revealed. Yes, there are the occasional Ernst Jüngers, who compared the exchange of hand grenades to a ballet and who counted his generation lucky to have been able to serve in such a great struggle, but the vast majority of the famous literature of the war, from Wilfred Owen to Siegfried Sassoon to Jaroslav Hašek, is a collective ode to futility, waste, horror, and despair. Is this, then, the truth?

In *The Fighters*, C. J. Chivers's superb book about the current American wars, he announces that he is rejecting senior officer views so that his book may channel "those who did the bulk of the fighting with the unapologetic belief that the voices of combatants of the lower and middle rank are more valuable, and more likely to be candid and rooted in battlefield experience, than those of the generals and admirals who ordered them to action—and often try to speak for them, too."

But of course, it's not just generals and admirals who try to speak for the common soldier, it's poets and novelists, too. Wilfred Owen is very self-consciously trying to speak for "his men," a move that, as the poet Tom Sleigh has pointed out, when contrasted with the less ideologically inflected (and, to my mind, artistically superior) work of an enlisted soldier like David Jones, can seem "at best . . . heroic posturing in an anti-heroic guise. And at worst . . . a form of unconscious class condescension." And many of the great writers to come out of World War I are writing in the emerging modernist tradition that had already, prior to the war, established itself in an iconoclastic

relationship with tradition and the old order. Filippo Tommaso Mari-
netti had demanded we "demolish museums and libraries" in 1909,
Ezra Pound had tried to move past the "crust of dead English" by
founding Imagism in 1912, Stravinsky and Nijinsky had shocked audi-
ences with *The Rite of Spring* in 1913. The spirit animating that generation of artists was revolutionary, tossing down old idols with reckless
abandon, and so we must ask: Were "honor, courage and patriotism"
revealed as lies by the war, or by these artists' commitment to the
prevailing current of thought among their tribe? Both, probably.

After all, the writings of those nonartists at war paint a more complex picture. As the historian Jonathan Ebel points out in the introduc-
tion to his *Faith in the Fight: Religion and the American Soldier in the Great
War,* "Soldiers' and war workers' writings do not allow the honest historian to write a polemical history or a predictable ideological cri-
tique. As much as one may love or hate the idea of war, love or hate
the men and women who plan wars and send others to die, love or
hate those who profit financially or politically from war, the voices of
soldiers and war workers will provide, at most, equivocal support."
And indeed, through soldiers' and war workers' letters and diaries he
finds that, though we now like to tell the story of World War I as
one of disillusionment, that was not the case for many Americans in
the war, who saw it as an opportunity to practice "Christianity of the
sword," by which they could find personal and national redemption
for a God-chosen nation—and that that narrative was strengthened
rather than weakened postwar.

Walter Poague, who flew seaplanes on antisubmarine missions
and who would be killed six days before the Armistice, wrote to his
mother, "This is not a terrible war. It is the most wonderful war in the
world. It is the war which means the real salvation of the world." Red
Cross nurse Elizabeth Walker Black noted the "exaltation about being

under fire" that shirkers "with their flabby souls and sluggish blood living selfish lives" would never get to experience. And infantry officer Vinton Dearing wrote to his mother of the strangely compelling nature of war:

> You go out into the moonlight and feel the place "holy and enchanted," a new world, half mystical, a different moon, more wondrous lights; then some tremendous 155 goes off and shatters your dream. . . . Life is great and the aims of the war are great. It is when you see into the aims with your inner eyes that you see the bigness of it all.

To which truth do we owe allegiance? If we accept Chivers's democratic notion that it is among the voices of lower- and middle-rank combatants where we find the truth of war, then our poetically informed ideas about World War I must get pulled in an uncomfortably militaristic direction.

As a writer who was once a Marine and writes about war, I am skeptical that there is any kind of final authority that we can rest on the supposed perspective of "the troops," whatever that might be, and doubly skeptical that such authority then reverts to artists. After all, the budding fascism of the postwar period can be spotted not simply among those who grimly clung on to a cold and fatalistic nationalism through all the bloody years of the war, but also among far too many disillusioned artists and writers, from Céline to Evola to Huelsenbeck to Pound. The destruction of the old values can lead in many directions.

Veterans and artists can convey to us the thrilling or horrifying or insane intensity of war experience. They can show us the desperate attempts at sense-making done by humans engulfed in it. They can allow war to revolt us or seduce us. They can lie, for sure, but even more dangerously, they can tell terribly impartial truths.

In the 1930s, Walter Benjamin took it upon himself to review a collection of essays, edited by Ernst Jünger, about World War I and the possibilities within German nationalism for those of "heroic spirit." As Benjamin, who a decade later would commit suicide while fleeing the Nazis, points out, all the authors "were themselves soldiers in the World War and, dispute what one may, they indisputably proceed from the experience of this war." And yet, despite this, and despite the fact when war broke out in 1914 Benjamin spent his time translating Baudelaire rather than fighting, he confidently, and accurately, condemns not only their work but even their ability to write about war itself. In the essay, titled "Theories of German Fascism," he declares:

> We will not tolerate anyone who speaks of war, yet knows nothing but war. Radical in our own way, we will ask: Where do you come from? And what do you know of peace? Did you ever encounter peace in a child, a tree, an animal, the way you encountered a patrol in the field? And without waiting for you to answer, we can say No! It is not that you would then not be able to celebrate war, more passionately than now; but to celebrate it in the way you do would be impossible.

This, it seems to me, rests authority where it ought to reside. Not in the lived experience of war, nor in the penetrating yet isolate truths of individual artistic geniuses, nor in the aggregated opinions of a given mass of veterans, but in a careful reader possessed of a vision of peace.

IV | FAITH

TALES OF WAR AND REDEMPTION

DECEMBER 4, 2017

W hen I was a kid, I had a comic book called *The Big Book of Martyrs*, part of a series by Factoid Books that included such titles as *The Big Book of Thugs*, *The Big Book of Losers*, and *The Big Book of Weirdos*. Inside the martyr book were comic-book depictions of various saints and their horrible, horrible deaths—great stuff if you're an eleven-year-old boy. I know that Catholics like myself are trying for a more modern, nicer Church these days, with less of the fire and brimstone and more of the let-the-children-come-unto-me, but I can't help thinking that if *Game of Thrones* can be a smash hit, then the Catholic Church might make progress in the ten- to fourteen-year-old demographic by leaning more heavily on the decidedly R-rated tales from *The Big Book of Martyrs*.

I enjoyed these stories immensely, but they were also confusing— and not because of all the killing and dying for faith. That, I could understand. God, on the other hand, behaved very strangely. He was always protecting His martyrs before their deaths, but (to my eyes) in what seemed like the laziest, most halfhearted way imaginable.

There's Saint Lucy, for example, who refuses to burn a pagan sacrifice. She is sentenced to be defiled in a brothel, but when the guards try to take her away, they find she's completely immovable. Big, muscular guards strain to drag off this slender young woman, but she's fixed to the spot, standing firm. Not the greatest miracle in the world but, okay, not bad. Then things escalate. They bring in a team of oxen, hitch her to the animals, and let them loose. Once again, nothing. Guards lash the massive beasts forward, the animals pull with all their might, but Saint Lucy does not budge. They lay bundles of wood at her feet and try to set her on fire, but the wood doesn't burn. Things are looking up for Saint Lucy. But then it's as if God gets distracted and looks away for a moment, while they rip out her eyes and stab her to death.

She's hardly the only one with a story like this. There's Saint Sebastian, protected from arrows only to be clubbed to death. There's Saint Agnes, who like Saint Lucy was ordered to be dragged naked to a brothel, though in her case God didn't make her immovable, he made thick, coarse hair sprout all over her whole body before some soldier beheaded her. Or Saint Cecilia, struck on the neck three times with a sword. Divine intervention enabled her to survive, which sounds great, but the miracle wasn't invincibility; the miracle was that somehow, despite a giant, bloody neck gash, she was able to walk around for three more days before dying of her injuries.

As miracles go, that has to be one of the shittier ones. If I'm going to die by the sword, I'd prefer to go quick, without the glorious and providential beneficence of the good old walk-around-bleeding-horribly-for-days miracle. Even the rapid-gross-body-hair-growth miracle is better than that.

For a boy, this is all highly entertaining and totally ridiculous. But as an adult, I came back to these martyrs when looking through a book of sermons from a medieval English abbot. There, in great detail, was one of those stories I'd previously read in comic-book form, the story of the Forty Soldiers.

Back in the days of the Roman Empire, there was a group of forty Cappadocian soldiers—noble warriors, loyal to one another in every fight, and always victorious in a raging battle. They were also Christians. This wasn't a problem until the empire appointed a new judge, Agricola, who loathed Christianity and decided to break the Forty.

First, Agricola ordered them stoned to death, but every time a Roman soldier threw a stone, it rebounded and struck him in the face. Soldiers kept throwing stones with the same result, until a magistrate picked up a huge flint and hurled it, only to have the stone rebound and crack open his head, at which point everybody decided stoning wasn't the best way to go.

The next day, Agricola ordered the Forty led in chains to a wide lake, covered in thin ice and whipped by rushing winter winds. The guards threw them, naked, into the center of the lake, and placed a tub of warm water off to the side, telling the freezing men that if they paid homage to the pagan gods, they could jump in and warm themselves.

That night, the lake froze, encasing the men and causing their flesh to break open from the frost. At this point, some of the men were likely wishing that God hadn't bothered to save them from stoning. One of the Forty broke and ran for the tub, only to die as soon as he touched the water. The rest of the men prayed to God in their suffering.

That's when the big miracle happened. All except one of the guards suddenly fell asleep. A heavenly light shone down, melted the ice, and made the lake's waters as warm as a bath. The one alert guard was so moved by this sight that he stripped off his clothes, rushed out to the lake, and declared himself a Christian. Then, true to form for a martyr story, the heavenly light stopped shining and Agricola ordered the legs of the Forty broken. They froze to death, and their bodies were burned.

My eleven-year-old self had seen this as yet another absurdity, another story of an absent-minded God, pulling His faithful out of the fire and forgetting about the frying pan. But to my surprise, reading it as an adult, I was moved, for the story made sense in a way I wished it didn't.

PART OF WHY begins with my chaplain in Iraq, Patrick McLaughlin, who was beloved by all of us at TQ, our forward operating base in Anbar Province. We called him Chaps. He was a tall, affable Lutheran, always ready with a smile or a joke. His most difficult duties involved TQ Surgical, our little combat hospital, which treated Marines, soldiers, Iraqi Army, Iraqi insurgents, and civilians. Given the amount of violence in Anbar Province at the time, this meant being witness to some pretty horrific things. The worst, for everybody, was seeing what war did to children.

Military triage is a cold, logical process. If there's no hope, you make the individual comfortable and move on to some other patient who might survive. But the doctors, who felt every loss keenly, would never just shove a dying person in a corner. They wanted someone to be there, caring for them until they passed. This was especially true when it came to children, and it was this responsibility that Chaps took upon himself. When there was nothing the doctors could do beyond providing morphine, Chaps McLaughlin used to hold kids in his arms and rock them gently as they died.

At first, he did this standing, or on his knees, outside the hospital. The first child was small, maybe six or seven years old, in the throes of agonal breathing, three or four respirations a minute—"ragged," Chaps described it to me years later in an email, "gasping, tiny chest heaving, lungs expanding as the mouth gulps air as though this breath is the very last and yet it's not." Chaps, a father of five, held that boy for an hour as he clung fiercely to life, his brains slowly seeping through his head, no family around to comfort him, the family unknown, perhaps dead. "When my nameless little boy died," Chaps wrote me, "I kissed his forehead."

For the second child, a three-year-old girl, her body tattered from an IED blast and half her face missing—a sight so awful that two of the medical staff, men long inured to every kind of injury, left the hospital to vomit outside—Chaps whispered calm words in her ear as a female corpsman, who had a daughter the same age, held her hand. It was after that girl passed that he asked the Seabees, a group of military engineers, to make him rocking chairs, "combat rocking chairs," the corpsmen called them, with which he could rock the dying children for as long as they held on to life.

Over the course of his time in Iraq, Chaps McLaughlin would rock eleven children in those chairs. Eventually, before redeploying, he took the chairs to a unit bonfire, threw them in, and watched as the embers rose heavenward to, as he put it, "the children that once occupied them in my arms."

My boyhood objection to the savagery of the martyrdom stories, to God's ultimate silence in the face of suffering and death, takes on a different light in the wake of such deaths. To anyone with any kind of experience in war, a story of God saving the good would feel less like a comfort and more like an indictment. Any soldier can tell you that no amount of prayer provides security for the defenseless in a war zone. The good die. The bad die. The combatants die, and the children die. The old men and the women and the fathers and mothers and sisters and daughters and sons die. Sometimes, often, they die horribly. When we return home, a new knowledge follows with us, the viscerally felt knowledge that men are cruel, that history is bloody and awful, and that the earth is a place where, no matter where you live, whether it's New York or Fallujah, Chicago or Baghdad, we are regularly failing to protect our most vulnerable, our poor, and our desperate.

We recoil at religious platitudes intended to get around this truth or to make it less bitter. So we can appreciate the way stories of martyrdom unrelentingly focus on suffering, refusing to suggest that faith might spare us from horror. The fourth-century Christians who first told the story of the Forty Soldiers knew that hard lesson better than we do. But that leaves us with the other piece of the story: the insistence on the miraculous in the midst of the suffering, the tales of pain as a means of inspiring us and drawing us closer to God, complete with dramatic miracles to underline the point.

The violence I have seen has left me feeling hollowed out, unable to gild all the agony with some beautiful meaning. As I watch the catastrophe that has befallen Iraq, it now seems absurd to cheaply suggest that it built toward any greater purpose, or paved the way for greater peace and prosperity, or that it is anything more than a net increase in the suffering and horror of a world awash in blood, or that there is even a realistic prospect for any kind of justice, some kind of restitution or payment or balancing out, even in a small way, for what has been erased.

In the modern era, we do not want to hear of death as a sacrifice, as an atonement or a gift. Religious claims are tenuous, and pain is certain. Pain provokes our sympathy, and our outrage, while hope of the resurrection serves as little more than a hypothesis. Ernst Jünger once declared pain the "authentic currency of our age." Perhaps this is why many consider it something of an embarrassment to speak of God in public, or to speak clearly and forthrightly of our experience of transcendence. We're much more comfortable talking about trauma. Physical trauma, done to bodies. Psychological trauma, done to minds. Something we can see when we look at a scar, or an MRI scan of the brain. That's hard data, not wishful thinking and willful naïveté. So we address ourselves to the suffering, which, after all, we can do something about. In the medical realm, we can seek cures. In the political realm, we can hunt those responsible. In both cases, we aim at suffering and leave questions of transcendence by the wayside.

MY TIME IN the Marines left that worn saying, "There are no atheists in foxholes," sounding especially hollow. For one thing, it's verifiably untrue. Marines come from every religious background. But even if we consider the adage's underlying meaning, that a man in enough terror will cry out to something, to anything, what kind of faith is that? The Russian journalist Artyom Borovik once described a young soldier in his first firefight, whispering to himself, as the bullets whizzed overhead, "Mommy, take me back inside of you. . . . Mommy, take me back inside of you." If this kind of impulse is the stuff of religious faith, then religious faith doesn't count for much.

A soldier may call out to God while in combat, but the experiences that caused him to do so might be the very ones that later cause him to abandon his faith altogether. What kind of God, after all, would allow any of the innumerable things that happen in a war zone?

This old complaint takes on a particular urgency when you've seen children dying slowly after going through more pain than any human being should ever experience. It's not even a complaint unique to war experience. When the writer Aleksandar Hemon's daughter was diagnosed with a rare brain tumor, he and his wife spent the next few months desperately trying to save her as she was subjected to chemotherapy, brain surgery, and rounds of drug treatments. She died anyway. The experience convinced him that the religious notion of suffering as somehow ennobling was a despicable lie. He later wrote:

> Isabel's suffering and death did nothing for her, or us, or the world. We learned no lessons worth learning; we acquired no experience that could benefit anyone. And Isabel most certainly did not earn ascension to a better place, as there was no place better for her than at home with her family. Without Isabel, Teri and I were left with oceans of love we could no longer dispense; we found ourselves with an excess of time that we used to devote to her; we had to live in a void that could be filled only by Isabel. Her indelible absence is now an organ in our bodies, whose sole function is a continuous secretion of sorrow.

So no, the most intense horrors of the world do not always lead to faith. There are plenty of atheists in foxholes, and some of them are atheists *because* of what they experienced in foxholes. It would be more accurate to say, as the Vietnam veteran Keith Nightingale has stated, that war leads less to faith than it does to a moment of choosing. Faced with immeasurable human suffering, causing immeasurable human suffering, causing the deaths of other men, experiencing the highest reaches of terror, fighting side by side with men you love so passionately you'd gladly give your life for them, only to see them killed or maimed—all this raises questions about the nature and purpose of life with an urgency that can't be held at bay by scrolling Twitter or turning on the television. Nightingale writes that the veteran thinks either "I have to believe in God who got me through this night," or "I cannot believe in a God who would permit what I have just lived through."

Karl Marlantes, the Vietnam veteran and author of the novel *Matterhorn*, argues that combat experience is inescapably spiritual. "Mystical or religious experiences have four common components," he writes: "constant awareness of one's own inevitable death, total focus on the present moment, the valuing of other people's lives above one's own, and being part of a larger religious community such as the *sangha*, *ummah*, or church. All four of these exist in combat. The big difference is that the mystic sees heaven and the warrior sees hell."

WHAT DID I SEE? As a public affairs officer, I was never in combat and never saw the hell that Marlantes did. Or rather, I saw a complex mixture of things. I saw civilians dealing with horrible injuries. I saw men dying in dusty combat hospitals. I saw men embittered by months without progress in a violent place far from home. I saw a unit coming to terms with the fact that it had accidentally killed two civilians in an escalation-of-force incident. But as the year progressed, I also saw Marines grow increasingly confident that they had changed Anbar Province. I saw markets opening. I saw Iraqi police chiefs boasting that they'd hunt down al-Qaeda in Iraq with or without our help. I saw a sheik reveal his bullet wounds to me and promise to fight those who'd done it. I saw police forces swell. I saw what I thought was a taste of victory. And of course, I saw far too many of those children. Once, I saw a one-armed girl come in with shrapnel wounds from a bomb that had just gone off. She hadn't lost the arm in that day's bombing; she'd lost it in a bombing a year before. She couldn't have been older than five, and this was the second time the war had shattered a part of her body.

In theory, this sort of thing should have forced the kind of choice Nightingale refers to. It certainly forced some brutal self-reflection for Chaps McLaughlin, who on Ash Wednesday of that year wrote in his personal journal, later published in the book *No Atheists in Foxholes*:

> As my anger boils over in righteous indignation, I know that none of us comes away clean—none of us walks away without blood on our hands—the blood of children on our hands from this war. . . . Being a noncombatant does not exempt me from one iota of responsibility. . . . Urban warfare means children living in fear, children in tears, children orphaned, children wounded, and—God forgive us all—children killed. I will have to square my presence here in Iraq—my life in the military—with my soul and my God.

That was Chaps McLaughlin's reaction, but he had actually held those children.

I was in a different position. My job in the Marine Corps meant that I was generally a spectator rather than an actor in the war. I was never faced with the responsibility of leading men in combat, never responsible for the direct act of killing, never faced with what Marlantes has described as "a situation approaching the sacred in its terror and contact with the infinite." Instead, I had the images of those children in my head, and for a young man, fervently believing in the mission and in the potential for the Marine Corps to turn around Anbar Province, they confirmed me in all I believed. A Special Forces veteran later told me why, for him, killing people in Iraq felt less morally troubling than killing people in Afghanistan. "Iraq may have been a giant clusterfuck," he said, "but al-Qaeda did always make it easy." In other words, al-Qaeda was so grotesquely, absurdly evil, you could not help but compare yourself with them and assume that you must be good.

So rather than challenging my Christian faith or provoking deep questions about who I was as a man, what kind of war I was in, and what sort of country I was a citizen of, the children made me feel like I didn't have to justify myself at all. When I got home, those children were a useful tool for propping up my image of myself as a decent human being. Confronted with a man who voiced contempt at the notion that anyone would fight in a war that had caused such horrendous civilian casualties, I told him, "I carried injured Iraqi children to medical care with my own hands! What have you done for Iraqi civilians recently? Posted snarky comments on Facebook?"

At the time, it was quite gratifying to suppose I'd come out the victor in a conversation about who has got the dead civilians on his side of the argument. Thanks to that feeling of certainty, that feeling of assurance that I was on the side of the good, questions of complicity fell away. I walked around like some bizarrely inverted, old-school Calvinist, assured of my own righteousness not because of any good I saw in my life, but because of all the evil I saw in others. My notion of the value of faith went away, convinced as I was that I could justify myself through events, through being on the right side in a political debate, through material things, and through the self-serving way I interpreted them.

ONCE, after a lecture I gave, a woman approached and asked me how to talk to her boyfriend. She pointed him out in the back of the crowd—a tall, good-looking guy with military bearing. "He's an Iraq veteran," she said, "and I know he had a really hard deployment. I know, during his deployment, something really bad happened, but he won't talk about it. It's this closed-off part of him. How do I get him to open up?"

I get this sort of question fairly often. For the spouses of men and women with trauma, war related or not, it can sometimes feel as though there's some mystery in their partner, some moment, a site of wounding. Maybe this veteran lost a friend, got IED'd, got shot at, experienced mind-breaking terror for months. Maybe it was something worse. There's this sense that, if only the partner knew what it was, they'd be able to move forward, that somewhere there's a key to understanding the loved one's pain.

But it doesn't work that way. There is no such key, no moment that once unlocked might be easily dispelled. I told her to focus not on the bad things he had been through, if she wanted to have that conversation with him, but on the good. Ask about his best friends in his unit, about the good times they had, about what he liked about the military, why he'd joined in the first place, about the bonds of love between soldiers, the sense of community and purpose. About all the things, in other words, that would give context and meaning to the bad things he'd suffered. We do not understand the oak tree through a clear picture of the scarred-over hatchet wound still visible in its bark. Trauma has less to do with a person than with how that person has grown around it. You cannot understand the harm that has been done without understanding the good suffusing the rest of life.

Evil seems so grand; good so quotidian. The drama of 9/11 is infinitely more impressive than the daily labor of placing one steel beam after another as you construct a building. There's a certain drama to the story of a child's death, while the day-to-day life of a parent raising a child—changing diapers, shopping for wet wipes, making baby food, and keeping to a strict schedule—is undeniably tedious. Yet it is that day-to-day work that shifted, for me, the meaning of those memories I had in my head of the injured children, shattered families, and lost lives.

On Memorial Day, I was sitting with my son in my arms, holding him, rocking him to sleep. The holiday is never a particularly happy day for me, but this was the first one I'd experienced as a father. I was looking at this little baby who hadn't let me or my wife sleep the night before, who had earlier peed on me and then laughed at my startled reaction, and I thought about how much we had already sacrificed for him in his first few months of life. How much we'd continue to sacrifice for him. How much love he'd brought into our lives, and how much joy, and how much joy he'd brought to the people around us, to his grandparents and uncles and great-grandparents and the rest of our family. How he'd enabled me to love the people around me in a deeper way. Then I thought about the violence and loss that had swirled around but never reached out and touched me directly while I was in Iraq. I thought about the Marines I'd known who died, but who now seemed like more than Marines, more like sons, like my son, loved, and I thought about the children in Iraq who were never given a chance at adult life. I considered them not as objects of suffering, not as the locations of wounds or as horrible images I can't get out of my head, but in much the way I view my son—as pure, transcendent, unbounded, fragile.

The birth of my son has changed me in many ways. I get less sleep, I'm even more disorganized than before, I'm more stressed out—and I expected those things. Before he arrived, I even had a small sense of the joy he would bring. What I did not expect was how much he'd deepen the sadness with which I view the world. These days I'm less capable of gazing on horror with a disinterested, intellectual curiosity. Less capable of employing suffering as a political argument without feeling that, in some way, the suffering makes a claim on me as well. That at the very least, it ought to leave its mark. I'm not saying you have to have a son to feel this—I think we all feel it to an extent—but for me, it was revolutionary.

The philosopher Emmanuel Levinas said that it is only when we come face-to-face with another person that we see the trace of God, that to look directly into another's face, not through a screen or photographic lens, inevitably leaves us with a sense of that other person as our responsibility, "to which," he writes, we are "wanting and faulty. It is as though [we] were responsible for his mortality, and guilty for surviving." If we accept that responsibility, hard to do with a stranger, though obligatory when it comes to your own son, it must necessarily change your life—and not simply because it provides you with onerous, unfulfillable obligations toward a suffering world, but because it connects you in a real way to that world and becomes the means by which you might find transcendent joy.

THESE DAYS, leafing through *The Big Book of Martyrs*, I no longer read those stories and think of the miraculous proclamations of God's glory as somehow waving away the harsh realities. It was the Gnostics who thought of the flesh as evil and the death of a believer as an escape from a material prison. For most Christians like me, who consider ourselves born into a universe made by God and proclaimed by Him as good at the beginning of Creation, accepting this world's joy is a part of our religion's mission. When the German theologian Friedrich Schleiermacher's only son died of scarlet fever at the age of nine, the grief-stricken father rejected calls for him to rejoice that his son was in heaven.

> Regarding this world as I always do, as a world which is glorified through the life of the Redeemer and hallowed through the efficacy of his Spirit to an unending development of all that is good and Godly; wishing, as I always have, to be nothing but a servant of this divine Word in a joyful spirit and sense: why then should I not have believed that the blessings of the Christian community would be confirmed in my child as well . . . ? Why should I not have hoped in the merciful preservation of God for him also . . . ?

In the Catholic tradition, it is that very sweetness of the world, a world Pope Francis urges the faithful to accept as "a joyful mystery to be contemplated with gladness and praise," that makes the loss more bitter, not less. This is the other piece of those ancient, fantastical stories I read as a child—the unfashionable, absurd, and magical way in which glory is constantly being revealed in the midst of suffering, the moments in which the clouds open, the frozen lake's waters become like a warm bath, and the one Roman guard capable of seeing this miraculous world for what it is reaches out toward joy, not pain, and in doing so joins the Forty in death.

The elements of the fantastic in those stories, the over-the-top miracles and wondrous deeds of the saints, I now think of less as foolish absurdities than merely unfashionable descriptions of a deeper truth.

G. K. Chesterton once asserted that fairy tales make us see the world more clearly than realist novels because they allow us to remember how strange the world really is. "They make rivers run with wine," he wrote, "only to make us remember, for one wild moment, that they run with water." To read a story in which we marvel at a fairyland in which the sky is green and the grass is blue serves to remind us that more marvelous, capricious, and delightful than this fantasy is the reality that the sky is blue and the grass green. We feel this most keenly when out in nature, walking across the ridgeline of a mountain—that sense of witnessing a grand cosmic drama in which we are an infinitesimally small part. In the stories of the martyrs, where the heavens are always opening up in glory or the sun blackening in sorrow, the world is not simply the stage for the moral drama of our lives and deaths, not merely a neutral setting for our joy and suffering, but part of revelation.

And it's when I think about that, and when I think about my son, that I realize maybe the hard-nosed realist view, the view that says it is the suffering that we must accept with a steely eye, and the abundant glory around us crying out from a supernaturally charged universe that we must look at with a patronizing, disbelieving smirk—perhaps that is the naïve view. Perhaps to misunderstand that is to misunderstand the source of our relation to such suffering.

I think of Chaps McLaughlin, holding one dying child after another, and the sense of brokenness that it left him with, and I think of myself, in my self-righteousness, and I realize it was not simply an acute sense of suffering I was lacking, but also an acute sense of joy with which to give that suffering context. You can accept the miraculous or not, the divine or not. Either way, we remain both blessed and guilty, obliged to absorb the full radiance of the world and to accept the consequences of our failings as people, as members of churches, as members of nations. To take our obligations to our fellow man seriously means knowing we will never be able to adequately respond. It means knowing, at all times, that we should be moving toward a revolutionary change of heart, for the strength to act more fully, directly, and powerfully in relation to the agony existing not just overseas, but in the divided communities where we live. It means knowing we will fail, and knowing the glory of creation is there for us anyway. It means accepting that being responsive to suffering and attuned to joy are not different things, but one and the same.

MAN OF WAR

NOVEMBER 11, 2018

I

It started in the middle of the night. The U.S. Army surrounded the buildings, established perimeters, and posted heavy weaponry at key positions, dividing the space around their targets into neat, geometric kill zones. But their targets were not terrorist hideouts—they were family homes. And so, instead of kicking down doors or blasting out locks with shotgun rounds, they knocked. They roused the families inside, woke husbands and wives, grandparents and young children. They pressed money into their hands and told them, "You have to leave. You have no choice. Pack." And then the soldiers stood in families' living rooms, watched as the families packed their things and left, carrying bags, sometimes leaving behind clothes and keepsakes in their haste.

Behind the army came the engineers. They built large earthen barriers, laid out concrete blast walls, placed sandbags around windows, set up radio and data connections to headquarters—in short, converted these former homes into small, defensible outposts. Where once children were raised, where husbands and wives argued and made love, there was now an armed camp of foreigners staring out from behind automatic weapons.

This was in April 2007, in a series of small towns south of Fallujah in Iraq. The people there had lived through the American invasion, through the multisided insurgency, through the growing consolidation of power by the Islamic State. Recently, someone had taken forty members of the towns, bound them, shot them, and left their bodies in a mass grave. And now the people who remained—poor, rural people—had new neighbors.

When they woke up, the physical geography of their towns had hardly changed, but the social geography had undergone an earthquake. The old power structure in those towns was the Islamic State. It had controlled towns and cities and smuggling routes and black markets. It had offered jobs and opportunities—forty dollars for laying a roadside bomb, more if that bomb blew up and killed or injured an American. It had offered the potential for a farmer or mechanic to work in an insurgent cell, rise up through the ranks, become a person worthy of power and respect. It had offered an ideological and religious appeal. It had offered a way to strike back at foreign invaders. And if you crossed it, it had offered torture and murder. Now it was being challenged.

But who, exactly, was challenging it? It may seem obvious that the American troops were the new power players in that region. After all, what was that night of forced displacements and rapid construction if not a show of power? A new boss was in town, and he wore an American flag on his sleeve, right?

That is what I thought at the time. I came in a military convoy two days later, looking out at the surrounding area from behind thick, bulletproof glass. When we arrived at one of these new combat outposts—COPs, they were called—I sat in on a briefing given by the leadership to discuss plans for moving forward. The essence of war is imposing order onto an inherently chaotic environment, and from inside the COP everything seemed very orderly, very controlled. We could look out at the surrounding town from towers covering every angle of approach with interlocking fields of fire. We had maps and satellite imagery and a Blue Force tracker that provided real-time data on the location of every friendly force in the region. We had an intelligence section that had mapped out every violent incident on every street and highway in the past couple of years. To the inhabitants of the town, perhaps, the changes we had wrought were bewildering and frightening. Perhaps they were looking on us in fear and confusion. But within the COP, behind our walls and weapons, stuffed full of data, sitting on some former townsperson's couch and listening to the briefing, there was no confusion. We could look out with what seemed like an objective, God's-eye view. We were in the town, of course, but not a part of it. The town was an object in our grasp. A text we could read.

But that feeling of power lasted only as long as you stayed inside the COP, surrounded by comforting maps and data. When it came time to leave, I walked outside the walls to where our vehicles were waiting and stood for a moment in the street. I looked at the Marines around me—performing their preconvoy checks on their vehicles and weapons—and then turned to the town surrounding us. There was a small road that intersected the main street we were on, and it ran straight for a bit before curving off into the distance. I felt a desire to start walking down that road, to just wander off from my unit and explore, a feeling somewhat akin to the odd desire one feels standing on a cliff or on top of a tall building, where that little voice whispers, perversely, "Jump."

This moment of vertigo was an intimation that, perhaps, we were not quite the new boss in town I imagined we were. Certainly, we had the most firepower. The greatest capability for effectively wielding violence. Simone Weil once defined "force" as "that x that turns anybody who is subjected to it into a thing." Under that definition, you could certainly say that we were the dominant force in the town. What is much more disputable, however, is whether we were the dominant power.

Power and the use of force are often conflated. "Power grows out of the barrel of the gun," said Mao. "Only violence pays," claimed Frantz Fanon. However, there is another, very different conception. "All governments rest on opinion," James Madison claimed, a statement that, as Hannah Arendt has pointed out, is as true for democracies as for monarchies and totalitarian states. In this conception, the strength of a society, and thereby the degree of power its government can wield, relies on the consent of the governed far more than on the constant, looming threat of violence. Indeed, states that rely on that constant threat, like North Korea, are notable for their weakness, their crippling need to internally police dissent to keep the house of cards from collapsing.

What to make, then, of my situation, staring down a dusty side street in a tiny, poor town bordered by desert? I knew that, no matter all the information we had—the maps, the Blue Force trackers, the intelligence reports and timelines of significant events—and no matter the tremendous show of force the town had just witnessed, there was not a single Marine or soldier behind me who would feel comfortable walking down that road alone. That simple physical space, a road in a town, the sort of thing that to me had always seemed no more than poured and hardened concrete, took on a new depth. That road was not simply a physical part of the geography, but the location of a complex social life, the setting for a set of relationships, customs, traditions, rituals, crafts, stories, songs, and practices. All of which, of course, were foreign to me.

None of these factors seemed important until I stepped outside the walls of the COP. They only exist as long as they are lived, and so they cannot be charted by a military intelligence cell, printed on a map, and pinned to a wall. Nevertheless, they barred me from the town as surely as our blast walls and earthen barriers excluded the town from our COP. They were not only real, they were dangerous. As Mao also pointed out, insurgents "move amongst the people as a fish swims in the sea." Walking through a town without having an intuitive sense of the people, then, could feel like driving in a foreign country at high speed down a narrow highway, full of dark turns over steep cliffs, and suddenly realizing that you don't know whether you're supposed to drive on the left or right side of the road.

II

In movies and on television, our recent wars tend to be portrayed in terms of violent action. Firefights and raids and slow-motion sniper bullets flying across the battlefield to kill the enemy. And it is understandable why. The exercise of violence, unlike the accumulation and use of power, offers a satisfying narrative structure. A raid is a morality play with a beginning, middle, and end, in which a set of brave warriors prepares for battle, strikes their objective, and ends the life of a bad guy. No wonder, then, that in our deeply unsatisfying, never-ending wars, the most popular cultural offerings are movies like *Zero Dark Thirty* and *American Sniper*, where we are treated to the spectacle of highly trained operatives killing undoubtedly evil people—bomb makers and torturers and sadists and thugs of all stripes—while the communities in which these fights happen are rendered almost invisible. In *American Sniper*, there is barely a civilian to be found—even the young children in that movie are actively engaged in trying to kill Americans—so the viewer need not worry about the complexities of waging war in and around people's homes. The city is not a social space but a hostile landscape that the soldier must dominate through brute force. And once the army has rampaged through the whole of the city, and the enemies have been killed or driven away, well . . . that is victory.

This can be fun to watch on television. The problem is that in real life, it often does not work. In the Second Battle of Fallujah, Marines and soldiers fought their way through the city, block by block. Close to two thousand insurgents, eight hundred civilians, and one hundred coalition forces were killed. It was the bloodiest battle involving U.S. forces since the Vietnam War. But by 2006 the city was once again firmly controlled by the insurgency. Aside from the structural damage visible everywhere, it was as if we had never fought our way through it at all.

And so, by the time I was in Iraq, the military had come up with a new strategy, formalized in the army's new counterinsurgency manual, U.S. Army Field Manual 3-24. This strategy emphasized knowing the cultural terrain, getting out and interacting with the people of your battlespace. "Sometimes," it cautioned, "the more you protect your force, the less secure you may be."

Some soldiers took this idea to extremes. In Afghanistan, Major Jim Gant, an officer in the Special Forces, would occasionally stop military matters to play with the local children in the town where he had been stationed. He later claimed, "I would play with the children—for hours. . . . I often thought that these play sessions did more for our cause in the Konar than all the raids we did combined."

The idea was to introduce a sociological, rather than purely physical, conception of security. And this is the reason I was in that little town south of Fallujah in the first place. An alliance of Sunni sheiks had decided, for a complex mixture of reasons, to oppose the Islamic State and cooperate with Americans. This alliance, the Anbar Awakening, had successfully leveraged the overwhelming force and wealth of the American military in their bid to upend the power structure of Ramadi. Insurgents were suddenly fleeing the city to rural towns. The next step, naturally, was to expand to those rural towns.

Hence the operation I went on, where the military had set up outposts to force U.S. units into close physical proximity with the people of Iraq. Terrifying the village and kicking families out of their houses in the middle of the night was, perhaps, not the most auspicious start, but the general idea was that, over time, living in little Iraqi towns, patrolling the streets, getting an intuitive feel for the life of the community they were supposed to police, the military would become more than just a looming violent force in the region, but a power player enmeshed in the life of the community. As Matt Gallagher, an Iraq War veteran who served during this time, put it: "So little of Iraq had anything to do with guns or bombs or jihads. That's what people never understand. There was the desert. And the locals, and their lives."

In practice, this meant not a series of clear-cut raids, in which good and brave soldiers kill bad and depraved terrorists and the world is made progressively safer one bullet at a time, but a series of complex negotiations whose success or failure depends on much more than the abilities of each side to conduct violence.

Here is an example: In 2010, a Special Forces officer named Ian Fishback was stationed in a section of Diyala Province when a group of Sunni tribesmen launched a few mortars at his base. Mortar attacks generally were not particularly serious—Major Fishback often slept through them—but in this case, the shrapnel from the rounds ripped out the throats of two service members, both of whom quickly bled to death.

Because of his knowledge of the area, Major Fishback was pretty sure he knew which tribe the mortarmen had come from and who was the local sheik nominally in charge. Most U.S. commanders would have, at the very least, arrested the sheik, interrogated him for information, and tried to bring people to justice. This is not what Major Fishback did.

He was operating in a volatile region and saw his job less as one of pacifying an insurgency than working out some sort of settlement between the competing groups that would allow them to live together peacefully. "The process was primarily political," he told me, "with violence in the background. Most of it was about reconciliation and politics. I don't think we ever killed anyone."

On the one side were the Sunni tribes, who felt threatened by Kurdish incursions into their territory. On the other were the Kurds, who had controlled that region until the late 1980s, when Saddam Hussein waged a genocidal campaign that killed up to 180,000 people and then resettled Sunni tribes in the devastated territory. The Kurds, understandably, were not particularly sympathetic to Sunni grievances.

And so, during his deployment, Major Fishback had served to open lines of communication between the various groups, operating as an outside force that could limit the uncertainty each side felt in negotiating with the other. He mapped out 550 nodes of power in the region, people with influence who could play a role in possible reconciliation, and he worked to help the local leaders build institutions that could, in the event of U.S. departure, help keep the peace. And he felt it was going well. He had sheiks who had fought in the insurgency for almost ten years and who had never met an American before who was willing to work with them. There was no descent into general violence. But then there were these mortar attacks. Two Americans dead. The sort of thing that requires a response.

Major Fishback called a meeting with the sheik whose men he thought were responsible, and the sheik agreed to come. Prior to the meeting, Major Fishback knew that the sheik probably had blood on his hands. He knew that the sheik probably knew who had launched the mortars, or at least knew enough to probably be able to help Major Fishback track them down. He also knew that the sheiks in the region did not have absolute control of their tribesmen, that the tribesmen often felt that attacking Americans conferred legitimacy, and that even tribal leaders who genuinely wanted to work with the Americans often turned a blind eye to the occasional mortar attacks, which rarely killed anybody and so were usually a harmless way for their men to get a shot in at the invaders. Usually.

"He came in, clearly very nervous," Major Fishback told me. "It was common practice among some people to detain sheiks during these meetings. But I was in the position of establishing the peace. Detaining him had the potential to undermine relations with the other Sunni sheiks. So I made it clear: If this happens again, we won't be friends. And he knew what that meant. The interpreter thought he was going to have a heart attack."

And that was it. Major Fishback made the decision to forgo a hard approach seeking justice for two needlessly dead Americans on behalf of the hope that continuing his relationship with the sheik would lead to better outcomes down the road.

This is not a great war story to tell at a bar. It does not have the clean trajectory of a sniper's bullet, the satisfying moral conclusion of the raid on Osama bin Laden's compound, or the awe-inspiring display of force that was the Second Battle of Fallujah. It is not even really possible to know whether it was the right choice, whether that particular sheik was as reconcilable as Major Fishback thought he was, or whether any of it really mattered in the long term. That year Iraq would have bitterly disputed elections followed by the Shiite prime minister going after Sunni politicians, igniting yet another round of vicious sectarian warfare in which ISIS was able to successfully woo the support of Sunni tribesmen.

Once you move outside the realm of physical force and into the realm of social power, you move into the realm of uncertainty. Each action of yours sparks a chain of reactions among the people you are trying to influence, reactions that all the social science in the world and all the mapping of nodes of power cannot predict. As Hannah Arendt points out, "The reason why we are never able to foretell with certainty the outcome and end of any action is simply that action has no end. . . . the smallest act in the most limited circumstances bears the seed of the same boundlessness, because one deed, and sometimes one word, suffices to change every constellation." There is no sure guide for action, no rule book that will tame a population, because populations are composed of free people with choices of their own to make. The exercise of power, then, means not dominating an external world but weaving yourself into a web of relationships in such a way that those around you begin making choices that take your wants and desires into account. This means that power, ultimately, is not about control. It is about submitting to a complex system that is out of any one person's control.

So Major Fishback cannot say for sure that he made the right choice, though he feels that he did. "I think it did well for the people," he told me. "I think it did well for the prospects for peace." Even if those prospects would not come to fruition.

When he left the area the Sunni sheiks cried. They told the Americans that the reason no one was killed was because of Major Fishback's team and the way the team conducted itself. On that deployment Major Fishback and his men had not killed anyone, had not exerted force and turned people into things; but in their own way, they had exercised power.

III

Major Fishback's work, however, was very different from my day job as a media officer. I ran a team of Marine correspondents, assisted professional media moving through Anbar, and served as an adviser on communications. Every morning, I had to brief my commanding general on the three biggest news stories out of Iraq, and in those early months they were never good. It was all chlorine gas attacks and assassinated political leaders and bombers using children as decoys. Eventually, the chief of staff called me aside and said, "Phil, you're doing good work, but . . . your morning briefings are kind of depressing. How about we add an extra, positive news story at the end of each briefing to, you know, pep things up."

This was the beginning of the Positive News Story of the Day, or, because the military loves acronyms, the PSOD, as it came to be called. I would have three horrible stories of violence and despair . . . and then tell the general, "But, for our PSOD, we have an article in *The New York Times* where John McCain says we're making progress."

Some days, though, the news was so overwhelmingly bad there

was almost nothing I could find. "No idea what the PSOD's gonna be," I'd tell my chief as I pored through the dregs of the internet, coming up with things so pathetically threadbare it was often worse to include them. "Well, sir," I'd tell the general, "we've got a suicide truck bomb that killed forty-seven people, the assassination of a tribal leader, a U.N. report saying that the Iraqi government has engaged in widespread torture, and, for our PSOD, from freedom-mom.blogspot .america.com, look at this adorable photo of a Marine who went on patrol and took a selfie with a baby goat."

I am not sure whether the PSOD ever made anybody in the briefing feel better about things. In fact, searching for a PSOD on a dark day was downright troubling. There were some times when trying to put a positive spin on a story felt obscene.

At one point during those early months, a Marine squad raided a house near my base where an execution was taking place. The insurgents had captured a couple of Iraqi soldiers, brutally beaten them, taken a power drill and drilled through their ankles, and then set them up in front of a video camera to be beheaded. It was then that the Marines burst in, killing or capturing the insurgents and freeing the Iraqis, who were given medical care and sent to the military hospital on my base.

A senior officer reached out to me and told me that this was a really dramatic story that spoke well of the American military, and I should head to the hospital, talk to the doctors, and see if one of the Iraqis was willing to do an interview about what he had experienced and how grateful he was to U.S. forces for saving him. And so, naïvely, I walked over to the hospital and asked to speak to one of the surgeons who'd worked on the tortured Iraqis. When I explained why I was there, it took him a moment to respond. This doctor, he had spent time with these men, with their broken bodies that would never be fully whole again. At first he did not quite understand what I was after. The notion that this was a good news story was inconceivable. It was one of the worst things he had ever seen in his life. Evil, written on the body. "You don't understand," he said in a strangled voice. "They're in really rough shape." I left, ashamed of myself.

IV

During this time, as I struggled through these emotions about myself and the place I was in and the work I was doing, I went to church and I went to confession. And in confession, I mostly talked about my sense of my own inadequacy. Here I was, in a site of deep moral concern. People were dying. People were being tortured to death. And I had joined the military to be of service. In high school the Jesuits had taught me to be a "man for others," the Marine Corps had promised me a way to do that, and so here I was. And yet, as a staff officer, especially as a staff officer with a job related to media, it was difficult to square my day-to-day activities with the life and death stakes all around me. I did not even know if I was helping or hurting the cause. Most of the journalists I hosted from major news organizations in those days tended to report only bad news. All I knew was that I had a safe job in a dangerous place, the sort of place where moral heroism was needed, and where I had not the slightest clue what that kind of heroism would even look like.

Faith, for me, has always been a place to register a sense of doubt, of powerlessness, of inadequacy and uncertainty about my place in the world and how I am supposed to live. You kneel before a crucifix. Before a broken, tortured, and humiliated human body. You face human frailty and human cruelty. You call to mind your sins. All that you have done, and all that you have failed to do, in a place where nevertheless you know you are accepted and forgiven. Those early days in Iraq were so busy it was easy to get lost in the constant flow of work. But my time at Mass, and particularly my time in confession, were when time stopped for me, and I tried to imagine ways of reordering myself in relation to this very disordered, broken world. Then I poured out my doubts, received reconciliation, and went back to my confusing day job.

However, on April 29, a week after I came back from those little combat outposts in those little towns south of Fallujah, *The New York Times* ran a story about the Anbar Awakening by Kirk Semple, a reporter I had briefly hosted. The article, "Uneasy Alliance Is Taming One Insurgent Bastion," was the first major piece of reporting from a reputable source on the Anbar Awakening, the alliance of Sunni sheiks that was reordering the power structure of Anbar Province. In it, Semple did a careful job of explaining what the Awakening did and did not signify, pointing out that the alliance was an uneasy marriage of convenience, that many of the sheiks had participated in the insurgency, that governance remained a wreck, and so on. The article ended with the suggestion that barring an eventual political settlement between the Shia-dominated national government and the Sunni tribes, the long-term effect of the Awakening might simply be to arm and organize a potential enemy to the Iraqi state. Nevertheless, he noted that in Ramadi the insurgency was on the run. At that time in the war, for an article in *The New York Times*, that was a PSOD. That was as PSOD-y as it got. And so my war started to turn.

Soon, more and more journalists were passing through Anbar Province, interested in covering the changes in Ramadi, or in the operation that would soon start in Fallujah. A steady stream of casualties still passed through our base, but it wasn't like before. Mortar attacks stopped. At a certain point, I could not remember the last mass casualty event. I saw fewer injured children. And I went from hope that we were winning to certainty.

It became a matter of statistics. How many patients coming into our military hospital? How many people dying in attacks across Anbar? Looking at the figures, it was easy to imagine a rough, utilitarian calculus in which my service was overwhelmingly justified by the changes wrought on the ground. It was, seemingly, an empirical question: Did fewer people die in Iraq because of the surge? If the answer was yes, then according to that strictly utilitarian, consequentialist calculus, I was right and noble, while the antiwar folks who opposed the surge were guilty of risking Iraqi lives.

Clausewitz, the great German philosopher of war, might have disagreed. For him, immaterial forces are often the most important forces in war; spirits that "seek to escape from all book-knowledge, for they will neither be brought into numbers nor into classes, and want only to be seen and felt." Since war is waged against "a living and reacting force," mechanical laws and rules will be "perpetually undermined and washed away by the current of opinions, feelings, and customs." Such arguments did not seem to matter at the time—the sheer power of the data suggested we had indeed found a rule book in which the spirits permeating war had been quantified and tamed. It would be only a few years, though, before those spirits would rebel and changing social and political conditions in Iraq would lead to the rapid collapse of the Awakening and the rise of ISIS.

But that was in the future. Not knowing the future, I knew the statistics. The numbers of the dead. The continual decline of violence. Statistics are wonderful. Like force, they turn people into things. For example, in January 2008, the last month I spent overseas, 554 Iraqis were killed. This is a horrible number if you think about it in terms of specific people. If you think of the woman with Down syndrome who on the thirty-first, the last day of that month, walked through a checkpoint to a pet market. She claimed she had birds to sell but, in fact, she had bombs strapped to her body, bombs she may not have even been aware were there. Within minutes, a remote triggerman detonated her in a flash of fire and blood and feathers. Survivors would describe awaking from the blast covered in blood, not knowing whether it was their blood or human blood or the blood of animals. One man searched for his friend Zaki among the various species of corpses until he passed out and woke up in a hospital bed. This incident left 46 dead. But when I thought of them, I did not think of the individual experiences and lives. I imagined a spreadsheet counting Iraqi casualties. A spreadsheet in which those 46 dead were numbers 482 to 527. A later blast, also from a bomb-carrying woman with Down syndrome, would bring the total for that month to 554. And when stacked against the previous January's 1,802 Iraqi deaths, this was a relatively low number. Which is the most pleasant way to think about it.

So I left Iraq, untroubled. Confident. I came home, untroubled, confident. Yes, soldiers had died. Yes, civilians had died. Yes, bodies had been torn and rent and I had even seen some of those bodies. There were images that stuck in my mind, like a man's eyeballs flattened and covered in reddened cloth. Like a father and mother holding an injured baby and looking on her with sorrow and love. Like a young Marine's tattoo as he lay on a trauma table. But from my secure vantage point as an officer, on a general's staff, following the big-picture news of the war, it was easy to anesthetize myself to such things, or to think about them in a sentimental, instrumental way. The soldier, whose name I did not know, was sacrificing for a good cause. The injured civilians, whom I did not know, were an example of why that cause was so good and our enemy was so evil.

In theory, war is supposed to enhance one's faith, or at the very least force a deep sense of reflection upon spiritual matters. The experience of war, and trauma more generally, can be an assault not only on one's physical sense of safety, but on one's social, moral, and spiritual conception of the world. Recovery, as the psychiatrist Judith Herman has described it, challenges the "ordinary person to become a theologian, a philosopher, and a jurist," who must reconstruct a view of faith, society, and ethics that will not merely collapse into the emptiness of the evil they have faced. Faith in God, faith in people, faith in the immaterial aspects of life that we rely on to go about our day-to-day existence needs to be rebuilt. And though many do not turn to God seeking aid in the process, for those who do, their faith can emerge stronger than ever.

But this was not my situation, which was comfortable, not particularly traumatic, and seemingly justified by external events—even if those events did not have much to do with my own actions. And so I stopped going to Mass. It was not a conscious decision. It would be a year before I would admit to a woman I was dating that I no longer believed in God. It was more that I simply stopped feeling the need to trouble myself about my spiritual life.

As the numbers went more and more in the right direction, I felt less and less as if I were in a place of mystery and confusion, but in a rational, controllable world where the correct application of right thinking and right technique could tame chaos, tame the wild spirits of war and civic life, and move us closer to a progressive, technocratically managed ideal of democracy and peace. I was less bothered by the war, by my place in it, and by the challenge of living justly in response to tragedy than by what I viewed as the shallow and wrongheaded political debates about the war back home and by the politicians I thought were lying about the facts—from Rahm Emanuel accusing

General David Petraeus of using "creative statistics," to Hillary Clinton suggesting it took "a suspension of disbelief" to accept what he was telling Congress.

My understanding not simply of the war but of myself shifted. I was not a fallen creature in a broken world reliant on grace, but a Marine in a successful army that had all the answers. I was justified not by a cross, but by an interpretation of public policy, not by the cruel and barbaric torture and murder of an innocent man, but by politics. If the surge had saved lives, turning a monthly death toll of 1,802 to 554, then the month of January did not just make me right and the antiwar folks who had opposed the policy wrong, it made me morally better than them by exactly 1,248 dead Iraqis.

It did not occur to me that I could be right about public policy and still be a sinner, or wrong about public policy and still be redeemed. And so I set aside the moments of doubt. I set aside the experiences that gave me pause. Like, for example, that moment I stood in that small Iraqi town, the town I thought I knew everything about, stared down a street, and heard a voice, my voice, saying: *I do not know where I am, or what I am doing, or what we are doing, and none of the Marines around me do either.*

V

In 2009, I left the Marine Corps and returned home. Very quickly, I developed a sense that something was missing in my life in New York. In an odd way, it was similar to that invisible force I had felt in that small town, the force that separated me from the town and its inhabitants.

Joining the Marine Corps, you see, is not just taking on a new job.

It is about entering an entirely different culture, one that in many ways echoes the nature and character of religious life. "Modern man may well find his monastery in the military," Samuel Huntington wrote in 1957, and I certainly found that to be the case. Like a novice monk, I was given new clothing, new standards of dress, a new haircut, as well as a distinct role within a broader community. I was given a list of virtues I was meant to embody—virtues like honor, courage, and commitment taking the place of the Christian virtues of hope, faith, and love. I went through rituals that mark the stages of life and the passage of power—swearing the oath of office, promotion ceremonies, award ceremonies, and, of course, memorial services. I was given a formalized language to use in chants and songs and shouted group responses. I was told that class, wealth, and race do not make a difference here. I was told to embrace austerity and mortification of the flesh. I was submerged into communal living, told that all were expected to give their bodies and their lives. I was given the stories of military saints—men and women who risked their lives under enemy fire, who jumped on hand grenades to save their buddies, who held faith with their fellow prisoners of war during years of torture. And the whole thing was sanctified with the blood of sacrificial figures, the fallen Marines who came before and gave their lives to the cause.

Out of the Corps, I was deprived of that community and not yet fully absorbed into the civilian world, which has its own rites and rituals and myths, many of them accepted unconsciously. I was alienated, as so many veterans have been before. There is nothing new or even especially dramatic about this. Plenty of veterans have come home and felt the same. Here are these incomprehensible people living absurd lives, without a thought in their head about the real world. And the real world, for some reason, did not mean the lives and families and hopes and dreams of ordinary men and women—it meant the war. It meant the stuff I cared about. As one Vietnam veteran put it: "I could not fathom how Vietnam could be anything to all Americans but the central concern of their lives; how it could be anything less than the dark sun around which we were all in unbreakable orbit as its doomed and somehow hopeless satellite."

To walk through a city like New York upon return from war, then, felt like witnessing a moral crime. Much as, in Iraq, we were frustrated that the Iraqis didn't just give up their own lives and goals and adopt our vision of a democratic society, I was frustrated, coming home, that the American people did not embrace my vision of war.

This was something I wanted to solve by writing fiction. I wanted to tell the oblivious American public what they needed to know. Here, my grand ideas were primarily psychological and moral and political. I thought I would write a novel about PTSD and thereby show a shamefaced nation what they had asked their Marines to bear. I would write about the dramatic suffering of soldiers and contrast that with the empty materialism of modern American life. I would write about the apathy of the broader American public about issues of war and peace. I, the authoritative returned veteran, would deliver my hard truths to a public that had failed in its civic duties. This was not about reconciling the civilian and military worlds, much less about reconciling the narrow experience of war within the broader social reality of the towns and villages where that war was fought, but about preaching from a great height.

It is somewhat amusing now that I thought, at the time, that those were the things missing from the public conversation. The public conversation in America at the time was full of those things, frequently written by people with a lot more knowledge than myself. But, like many young writers, I was eager to regurgitate the culture back at itself.

So that was one motivation. But there was another, messier motivation that I could not quite have articulated at the time. It was less about a message to unload upon my reader, and more about a group of unquiet memories that hung around in my head, cluttering up the place without serving as fodder for an easily digestible moral of the sort I wanted to impart. They were memories like the following: how funny it could be to talk about dead bodies, what it looked like seeing dirty soldiers back from a patrol eating cherry cobbler in the TQ mess hall, the voice of that doctor as he told me what it had felt like treating those two tortured Iraqis, watching a man shepherd a group of sick sheep with mucus hanging from their snouts, and the adjustments men made in the summer months to deal with ball sweat.

And because I was writing fiction, and not weekly opinion pieces, the odd, unquiet memories began to win. Fiction is strangled by simple messages, by notions of justice dependent on statistics where, as Gabriel Marcel put it, every individual is "reducible to an index card that can be sent to a central office." Or, he might have added, to Facebook's algorithm. But fiction thrives on sick sheep and ball sweat. Stories are things that happen not to ideas or statistics but to people, people with bodies, living in specific places. And so, unconsciously, and simply by the form that my writing took, I began to undermine my own certainty.

Around this time, people I knew were injured. A few people I respected were betrayed by the Marine Corps, treated badly and callously and cruelly. A few Marines I knew and liked experienced periods of homelessness. A bitterly disputed parliamentary election in Iraq threatened recent security gains. And so, without quite knowing why, I went back to Mass for the first time in years. And I thought about how the world was not quite meeting my hopeful expectations. And Christ, looking back at me from the cross, blood dripping from the thorns in His crown and the wound in His side and the nails in His hands and feet, asked, "What on earth convinced you that it would?"

VI

In the book of Job, after the hero has been stricken with illness, suffered the death of his children and his servants, he asks to make his case before the Lord, to ask what he has done to merit such suffering. And the Lord does respond to him, speaking out of the whirlwind. But instead of giving him answers, God offers rhetorical questions. At first, they are about what Job knows of the world—"Where were you when I founded the earth? Tell me if you have understanding. Who determined its size? Who laid its cornerstone?" And then God switches to a set of questions about what Job can do, what he can control, if he can thunder with a voice like God's, if he can humiliate the proud, bury them in dust. And God ends with the famous image of the Leviathan, later used by Thomas Hobbes as an image of the state itself, that vast conglomeration of people that form a civic body. God asks:

Can you lead Leviathan about with a hook,
or tie down his tongue with a rope?
Can you put a ring into his nose,
or pierce through his cheek with a gaff?
Will he then plead with you, time after time,
or address you with tender words?

Will he make a covenant with you
that you may have him as a slave forever?
Can you play with him, as with a bird?
Can you tie him up for your little girls?

It increasingly seems to me that the certainty of earlier life was based on fantasies of an orderly future in a rational, controllable world, fantasies that were no more than the wish that the Leviathan might one day be tied down by force. That man, with his ever-increasing sophistication and technology, could come up with a set of rules about how states are to be built, how societies are to be governed, how men are to be made to live, that would allow us to lead the Leviathan of the state, the city, or the town with a hook, tie its tongue down with a rope, and make of it, and men, a slave.

And so, though I struggle with faith, faith not only in God but in my country, my Church, and my fellow men, I go to Mass. I return to doubt, and confusion, and uncertainty. I return to a social gathering. To a meal. To the experience of music, to the image of our tortured God, to the recitation of words. To that moment when everybody in the church trips over the phrase "consubstantial with the Father." To the hands of my fellow congregants offering me peace. To the inscription of the sign of the cross on the forehead, lips, and heart. I return to the physical expression of a broader social body that proclaims itself a mystical body, each one of us branches emanating from the vine that is Christ. I return to a place designed to pull me out of my individualistic American brain and situate me back inside my skin, and inside a community, with all the raucous contradictions and odd harmonies that implies.

Paul tells us "the Kingdom of God is not in word, but in power." And at times, I think I can feel that power around me. Catholicism is not, or should not be, a religion of force. Not of hard mechanical rules, but of stories and paradoxes and enigmatic parables. It is an invitation to mystery, not mastery, to communion, not control. It is a religion that fits with what I know of reality, that helps me live honestly, and that helps me set aside my dreams of a less atavistic world in which men follow rational orders and never rebel. Perfect obedience, after all, comes not from men, but machines. Fantasies of control are fantasies of ruling over the dead. And my tortured God is not a God of death, but of new life.

CAN THE TRAUMA OF WAR LEAD TO GROWTH, DESPITE THE SCARS?

JULY 6, 2020

The French weapon deployed against Spanish troops in 1521 was, contemporaries said, "more diabolical than human." The rapid-firing light bronze cannon shot iron balls that crushed battlements, careened wildly, and sprayed shards of stone in all directions. At the Battle of Pamplona, one cannonball twice injured the leader of a small Spanish garrison defying calls for surrender, nearly killing him, first by striking one leg with stone shrapnel, then the other leg with the cannonball itself. His name was Íñigo López de Loyola. The effect on Loyola was not only physical, but also spiritual: Today, he is better known as Saint Ignatius.

Back then, he was no saint. One biography describes him as "a rough punkish swordsman who used his privileged status to escape prosecution for violent crimes committed with his priest brother at carnival time." But this near-fatal injury changed him, along with a few religious books he read during his exceptionally painful convalescence, in which his bones had to be broken again and reset, and where he came so close to death he was given last rites. He went on to found the Jesuits and send disciples all over the globe, in what the British historian Dom David Knowles suggested was Christianity's "greatest single religious impulse since the preaching of the apostles."

When we speak of trauma, it is usually as something to be avoided at all costs. "Interest in avoiding pain," wrote the utilitarian philosopher Peter Singer, is among "the most important human interests." And yet soldiers like Saint Ignatius, who found in their suffering a strange and terrible blessing, are not rare. Senator John McCain, brutally tortured at the Hanoi Hilton, famously declared himself "grateful to Vietnam" for giving him "a seriousness of purpose that observers of my early life had found difficult to detect."

His might be an extreme case, but the expectation of exposure to some trauma has long been part of the draw of war. "The law is this: no wisdom without pain," wrote the ancient Greek playwright and military veteran Aeschylus. "Wanted or not by us, such wisdom's gained; its score, its etch, its scar in us goes deep." Perhaps that's true, but it leaves us with an ugly and, to some, offensive question: Can suffering be a gift?

In the early twentieth century, Ernst Jünger, who had proudly served four years in brutal frontline fighting in World War I, declared the answer was a resounding yes. "Tell me your relation to pain," he claimed, "and I will tell you who you are!" Civilization before the war had slid into bourgeois decadence, he thought, fleeing from self-sacrifice and prioritizing safety. But the war heralded a new sort of man.

"Hardened as scarcely another generation ever was in fire and flame," he wrote of himself and his fellow soldiers, "we could go into life as though from the anvil; into friendship, love, politics, professions, into all that destiny had in store. It is not every generation that is so favored." Postwar Germany convinced him that the industrialized world these men returned to, which happily destroyed workers' bodies for the construction of railways or mines, was ruled by the same cruel logic as the trenches. Men would have to rise to the challenge by accepting pain, and accepting the cruelty of the age. This is toughness and callousness elevated to a first principle. Unsurprisingly, many of Jünger's admirers became Nazis.

One of their victims was an Austrian of Jewish descent named Jean Améry, who after the war forcefully rejected, in the starkest terms, any notions of suffering as a gift. Likewise, notions of stoic detachment born of the trenches were absurd to a man who had been tortured by the Gestapo before being sent to Auschwitz. Améry experienced pain beyond description; he was hung by his arms until they ripped from their sockets, and then horsewhipped. For the tortured man, he wrote, "his flesh becomes total reality."

More lasting than the pain, though, the experience destroyed his ability to ever feel at home in the world, which requires faith in fellow men. Humans are a social animal, our inner self in constant outward search for communion. Torture inverts that expansive, capacious self into a collapsing star. Whatever you thought you were—a mind, a consciousness, a soul—torture reveals how simply, and casually, that can be destroyed. "A slight pressure by the tool-wielding hand is enough," Améry wrote, to turn a cultured man into "a shrilly squealing piglet at slaughter." There is wisdom here, though of a dark sort. "Whoever was tortured, stays tortured." Améry committed suicide in 1978.

Where does that leave those who suffer? For the medical community, the safest option is addressing symptoms, not metaphysics. The writer and former Marine infantry officer David J. Morris has described his own therapy for post-traumatic stress disorder from his time in Iraq, during which he was urged to retell the stories of his trauma, practice breathing exercises, and reframe his cognitive responses to his environment and his traumatic memories.

But he was not encouraged to grow in response to what he had gone through; when he would try to speculate on how his experience might be converted to wisdom, psychologists would admonish him, he reported, "for straying from the strictures of the therapeutic regime." One senior psychologist at the Department of Veterans Affairs told him that notions of post-traumatic growth were an insult to those who have suffered. For a medical community grounded in science rather than spirituality, and rightfully leery of telling the Amérys of the world to look on the bright side, suffering is no gift.

But another current can be found in theories developed during the Vietnam War. The study of psychological trauma suffers from what the psychiatrist Judith Herman has called "episodic amnesia," in which periods of active interest, frequently following wars, are followed by "periods of oblivion." But the generation of soldiers disaffected from war during Vietnam organized and demanded the first systematic, large-scale investigations of war trauma's long-term effects. In addition to a medical diagnosis—PTSD was added to the American Psychiatric Association's official manual in 1980—many of these same veterans and their allies argued for the spiritual and moral significance of their condition.

Psychiatrists like Robert Jay Lifton and writers like Peter Marin argued that the suffering of Vietnam veterans was not simply neurosis, but appropriate moral response to horror. "All men, like all nations, are tested twice in the moral realm," Marin wrote. "First by what they do, then by what they make of what they do." Rather than numbing themselves to pain, they needed to sensitize themselves, to become alive to the "animating" guilt they supposedly lived with. Guilt forces the suffering consciousness outside of itself, the theory goes, sparking empathy and a drive to make reparation.

Whether guilt results in healing, though, is debatable. Some of the most fascinating research on growth after war trauma emerges out of a four-decade-long study initiated by Zahava Solomon, which followed the PTSD trajectories of veterans of the 1982 war in Lebanon and the Arab-Israeli war of 1973, also known as the Yom Kippur War. A 2016 analysis of Israeli POWs from the 1973 war, who faced systematic torture, deprivation, and social stigma, did find that those who reported the most guilt about their experience also reported the most growth. However, those veterans also had greater reports of PTSD symptoms as well. As Aeschylus warned, the wisdom they felt they had gained came with deep scars.

None of this would likely have surprised Ignatius of Loyola. In his tradition, suffering was at best a mystery: God never really answers Job, and Christ's prayer to "let this cup pass me by" goes ungranted. As a Jesuit friend recently told me, suffering is never a gift, never truly willed by God; suffering is real, and awful, and not to be forgotten. "Consider how the Divinity hides Itself," Ignatius's followers have been directed to ask for hundreds of years, "how It could destroy Its enemies and does not do it, and how It leaves the most sacred Humanity to suffer so very cruelly." But of course, that doesn't mean that we cannot respond to such suffering with grace.

AMERICAN PURPOSE AFTER THE FALL OF KABUL

SOLDIERS WERE TOLD THAT WE WERE CHAMPIONS OF THE RIGHTS OF MANKIND

AUGUST 25, 2021

There's a story that Marines tell—I've heard it more than once, in slightly different forms, and it goes something like this: Years into the war in Afghanistan, a squad of Marines heads into a remote village in the mountains. When they arrive, at first the villagers mistake them for Russians. When they explain, "No, we're American," the villagers ask, "Why are you here?" One Marine I met claimed to have initially been stumped by the question. It was 2010, he recalled. Why *were* we there? He said that he ultimately responded to the villager that some bad people who lived here flew planes into buildings and the buildings fell down. At which point, the villagers looked at one another in utter confusion. No one who lived there, they were certain, had ever been inside a plane, let alone flown one.

The story is told with a grin, like it's a joke. That's how you know it's deadly serious. Look at this ridiculous war, the Marine is telling you, and look at me, with my American flag on my shoulder, trying to make sense of it. It suggests the element of the American psyche that Ralph Ellison called "an ironic awareness of the joke that always lies between appearance and reality."

Since the fall of Kabul, though, the gap between appearance and reality has shrunk, bringing many long-running jokes to an end. The joke of generals boasting about how much progress has been made training the Afghan army. The joke of the intelligence community predicting how long the Afghan government could resist the Taliban. The joke of our promises to Afghan allies that, if worst comes to worst, we'd protect them, give them visas, and reunite them with their families somewhere safe.

Instead, the Taliban walked into cities unopposed; the president of Afghanistan fled the country; and crowds of desperate Afghans surrounded an American C-17 cargo plane as it took off from Kabul, some so desperate that they clung to the landing gear as it lifted. Videos show an Afghan falling from the sky. News reports tell of human remains later found in the wheel well of one of the planes.

How does it feel, as a veteran who watched the Iraqi province where I served fall to ISIS, to now watch this country—where Marines I knew were shot or blown up or killed—fall to the Taliban? Who cares? As the Taliban go house to house looking for those Afghans who believed in us and had the physical courage to put that belief to the test, who cares how I feel? Who cares how the vets who battled alcohol addiction only to start drinking again this week are feeling? Who cares what my Marine friends are feeling as they receive frantic text messages from Afghan allies? Not, for sure, Americans over the last twenty years.

"Everyone wants to know, am I OK, and I'm like, 'Really?'" a friend who served in Afghanistan during Obama's brief surge told me. "Is the burden of feeling guilty about this also a burden veterans have to carry, too? Not only did you not care about Afghanistan, not only did you not follow Afghanistan, it's like you gave such a little shit you can't even feel bad yourself? Could somebody else please take some of this, take some responsibility? I'm so fucking tired of it and it's killing me and it shouldn't be fucking me up this much."

Dane Sawyer, a veteran who served with Afghans in an Army civil affairs unit, wrote to me of his effort to save Afghans: "I have had no success despite all of the forms I've completed, phone calls I've made, and emails I've sent. It feels oddly familiar." He's been working with a family of eight who have been camping outside the Kabul airport for four days, with a family near Herat sending messages every morning asking whether they can go to Kabul, with a single mother waiting in Kabul for a call to go to the airport, and others. "I wish I could turn a blind eye, but the messages I am getting are so utterly desperate and harrowing, but I know soon I will have to just tell people there is nothing more I can do."

But I don't want to talk about how veterans are feeling now. And it's not for me to say how Afghans are feeling, or what America looks like to them as the C-17s lift off and leave them behind. I want to talk about how Americans felt, twenty years ago, when all this began.

I don't have sharp memories of the attacks themselves, in part because I mostly missed them. I'd been in the woods, disconnected, cheerfully oblivious while the whole nation watched the buildings go down again and again on television, uncertain of what could happen next, of how many more planes were in the sky, what other buildings were about to be hit, and who else might die. When I emerged from nature, the national mood had reached a fever pitch. There was grief mixed with fear and rage, yes, but there was something else. Something dangerously seductive. America had found moral purpose again.

Soon, George W. Bush's approval rating was more than 85 percent, Rudy Giuliani was "America's Mayor," and overseas, America was a subject of sympathy and support. I've heard people speak almost wistfully of those days. If you weren't a Muslim being harassed or spied on by the police, it was easy to feel a deep sense of connection to your fellow citizens, a pride in being American, and a knowledge that we'd get through this, we'd grieve, we'd rebuild, we'd get revenge, and we'd change the world in the process.

Let's admit it: those days felt good. Not for my friends who lost family in the attacks. Not for the woman I know who barely made it out of the towers and has spent the past twenty years wondering why she survived and so many of her colleagues did not. But for most of the rest of us, our country was justifiably at war. War with noble purpose. "Afghanistan is being, if anything, bombed OUT of the Stone Age," quipped Christopher Hitchens. A brutal Taliban regime was ending. Women were going to school. Men were shaving their beards and looking in astonishment at their naked faces in the mirror. No wonder Iraq, suffering under the boot of a truly evil dictator, began to look inviting.

A buddy of mine, the journalist and veteran Jacob Siegel, recently admitted to having an instinctive recoil against men our age who didn't serve in the military. "It's unfair, but I feel that," he said. "Who excused you, you know? Or another way of putting that would be, Why did you think you had a choice? I know it's a volunteer army, but the volunteer army is a trick question, you know? You're supposed to say yes if you have any honor."

More of us veterans feel that than we publicly admit. The voice in our heads whispering, If you had honor, you joined. You went to make the world safe. To plant peace in long-suffering nations, with no selfish ends to serve, desiring no conquest, no dominion. We were told that we were the champions of the rights of mankind.

The next time that feeling comes around, remember what it wrought. 9/11 unified America. It overcame partisan divides, bound us together, and gave us the sense of common purpose so lacking in today's poisonous politics. And nothing that we have done as a nation since has been so catastrophically destructive as what we did when we were enraptured by the warm glow of victimization and felt like we could do anything, together.

ACKNOWLEDGMENTS

Writing essays is, even more than for fiction, a group effort. My wife, Jessica Alvarez, is normally the first line of defense when it comes to guarding the world from bad prose and poorly thought out ideas. There have been many, many busy nights when, after a hectic day, I've asked her to read yet another draft and help me find what's wrong with it. There are many friends who have been equally selfless in this regard, especially Matt Gallagher, Elliot Ackerman, Christopher Robinson, and Jacob Siegel. Then, of course, there are the many editors and fact-checkers at various publications who have helped shape these pieces. There are so many people I've worked with over the years that I'll inevitably fail to note each one, and I apologize in advance.

Peter Catapano at *The New York Times* edited and published my first essay, "Death and Memory," in a section of *The New York Times* website called Home Fires. This was where Peter published many other veteran writers trying to make sense of the wars, and so I am not simply grateful for his always-thoughtful editing and conversations about possible pieces (I have written for him many times, including five of the pieces here), but I am also grateful for the rich variety of veteran writing he shepherded into print and on the web, providing a space for a vital dialogue about war that was deeply important to the veteran community as a whole.

Other editors I have been grateful to work with include Dan Saltzstein, Lucas Wittmann, Harry Siegel, Joshua Rothman, Joshua Greenman, Bruce Falconer, Strobe Talbott, Beth Rashbaum, John Swansburg, Jennifer Orth-Veillon, Julius Krein, Mike Madden, David Rhode, Lauretta Charlton, Kerry Weber, Warren Bass, and others.

Finally, there is my editor at Penguin Press, the great Scott Moyers, as well as my agent, Eric Simonoff, whose input and friendship have been invaluable over the past decade. Many thanks to Mia Council for her help as we were putting this together, and to the wonderful Jane Cavolina, who provided a final copyedit.

The John Simon Guggenheim Memorial Foundation and Princeton University's Lewis Center of the Arts Hodder Fellowship provided me the time and resources to write and research, and I very much hope to justify their faith in my work. Many thanks as well to John Ptacek, who provided invaluable research assistance through Hunter College's Hertog Fellowship program, and who was both an excellent researcher and wonderful conversation partner on everything from medieval saints to modern human rights work. Many thanks also go to all the scholars and experts who gave their time for the interviews that informed these various essays.

I'd like to thank my parents, Marie-Therese and William Klay, and my mother-in-law, Adriana Velásquez, for love and support and occasional help with childcare. I'd like to thank my sons Adrian, Marcos, and Lucas Klay for so many things, but most of all for giving me the best of all possible reasons to hope for a better world.

INDEX

INDEX